Bicycling the Blue Ridge

Bicycling the Blue Ridge

A Guide
to the Skyline Drive
and the Blue Ridge Parkway

by Elizabeth and Charlie Skinner

Menasha Ridge Press
Birmingham, Alabama

Copyright © 1990 by Elizabeth Skinner and Charlie Skinner

All rights reserved
Printed in the United States of America
Published by Menasha Ridge Press
Second edition

Library of Congress Cataloging-in-Publication Data

Skinner, Elizabeth, 1961-
    Bicycling the Blue Ridge: a guide to Skyline Drive and the Blue Ridge Parkway/
by Elizabeth and Charlie Skinner.
—1st ed.
     p. cm.
    Includes bibliographical references and index.
    ISBN 0-89732-093-X
    1. Bicycle touring—Virginia—Skyline Drive—Guide-books.
    2. Bicycle touring—Blue Ridge Parkway (N.C. and Va.)—Guide-books.
    3. Skyline Drive (Va.)—Description and travel—Guide-books.
    4. Blue Ridge Parkway (N.C. and Va.)—Description and travel—Guide-books.
    I. Skinner, Charlie, 1943- . II. Title
    GV1045.5.V82S626   1990
    796.6'4'097559—dc20   90-6572
                                                        CIP

Menasha Ridge Press
3169 Cahaba Heights Road
Birmingham, Alabama 35243

For Rosamond Foltyn and Anne Cornwall Johnson

In Memory of Willis David Johnson

Contents

Acknowledgments

We would like to thank the exceptional people who helped make this book possible. We are indebted to our family for their love and support.

Our good friends, Kathleen and Fred Wheeless, served as sounding boards for our ideas and provided needed assistance with photography.

The Forsyth County Public Library System was an invaluable resource and a generous employer.

We are grateful to Jeff Patton, Associate Professor of Geography at the University of North Carolina at Greensboro, for providing his time, expertise, and patience in developing the elevation profile maps.

Kate Dunlap and Laura Mansberg were both instrumental as editors. The manuscript most definitely matured through their impetus.

Anne Kennedy joined the Menasha Ridge staff just in time to add her sunny outlook to the final stages of the production process.

A final thanks goes to Jessica Letteney, production manager of Menasha Ridge Press. Thanks for being in our corner.

Preface

There is no ribbon of highway more ideal for bicycling than the Skyline Drive and the Blue Ridge Parkway. Perhaps we feel this way because we stubbornly seek out roads that are at once enticing to the senses and physically challenging. We both spent the greater part of our lives in Florida, a state summed up by bicyclists as hot, flat, and full of headwinds. There is no fall season in Florida. It's pretty much green there year-round. So, bicycling against a backdrop of yellow, russet, and orange was a new experience for us. After five years of exploration by bicycle, the Blue Ridge continues to amaze us.

Now let us concede from the beginning, the Skyline Drive and Blue Ridge Parkway are never easy. You simply cannot be a passive cyclist on these roads. You work excruciatingly hard climbing its mountains. But the descents are more thrilling than your favorite roller coaster ride. They're scarier too, for the controls are all yours. All senses are alert. Body and machine meet rubber and pavement in a high voltage connection.

Cycling on the Skyline Drive and Blue Ridge Parkway can be a humbling experience. The bicyclist who attempts these roads has definitely signed up for some tough mountain cycling. If the worst hill you've tackled is that bridge or overpass in your otherwise flat hometown you are in for a big shock. We'll address this matter of hill climbing later. First, a word about what motivated us to write this book.

In our travels on the Skyline Drive and Blue Ridge Parkway we have met cyclists from France, Japan, California, Florida, Texas, all in varying stages of bewilderment and frustration. The Skyline Drive and Blue Ridge Parkway present special challenges to the cyclist. In addition to steep road grades, weather conditions are often a menace. Rain, fog, and gusty winds are all possible. Facilities are set up for the convenience of the car traveler. Food stops may simply be too far apart to be practical for the bicyclist. Since the Park Service allows no advertising on the Skyline Drive and Blue Ridge Parkway, motels, restaurants, medical facilities, and the like are often obscured from the cyclist.

Facilities as close as a half mile off the Parkway may be completely hidden from view. Even the literature that outlines facilities off the Skyline Drive and Blue Ridge Parkway is almost exclusively designed for the car traveler. We have learned the hard way about turning off the Parkway only to find ourselves in an immediate descent to nowhere. This means only one thing: a tough climb back up the side of a mountain. And we like to climb. If only there were a traveler's guide written for bicyclists from the point of view of bicyclists.

We wrote this book with three groups of bicyclists in mind: racers, long-distance touring cyclists, and recreational cyclists. The Blue Ridge Parkway and Skyline Drive have much to offer each group. Of course, many bicyclists cross over between categories.

Overall, this book is designed for the touring bicyclist who plans to do the Skyline Drive and the Blue Ridge Parkway in an extended tour. In our view, this approach maximizes the experience. However, nothing is more gratifying than a hard ride with just you, your racing bike, and the mountains. No gear, no hassles. We live in Winston-Salem, North Carolina, and a single Sunday ride on the Blue Ridge Parkway can sustain us at least until the next weekend.

If you are a racer, you may not care about campgrounds and motels, but you probably appreciate knowing where the country stores and other food stops are. We can think of no better training ground for a racer than these roads.

Part of the fun of bicycle touring is making discoveries along the way. We do not want to take any mystery away from this. Our hope is that this book can enhance your experience. You, as the touring cyclist, still have the excitement of coming upon the delights of the area; but perhaps you won't find yourself famished because of a ten-mile miscalculation over the next food stop. Glendale Springs Restaurant and Inn is only a half mile from the Parkway, but you would never know of its gastronomic promise as you cruised past Milepost 260.

Disclaimer

Bicyclists assume responsibility for their own safety each time they undertake a bicycle trip. No guidebook can alert you to up-to-the-minute changes in weather, traffic, and road conditions. Each cyclist should consider his or her own abilities when planning a bicycle tour of the Blue Ridge. *We strongly urge you to wear a helmet.*

May all of your cycling adventures be safe and bursting with fun, thrills, and excitement.

Part 1:
An Introduction
To Bicycling in the
Blue Ridge

1 The Ultimate Bicycling Road

For the bicyclist, the Blue Ridge Parkway and Skyline Drive present an impressive list of statistics. Taken together, these two highways comprise 575 miles of continuous road which rides the crest of the Blue Ridge Mountains. The Blue Ridge Mountains are the eastern rampart of the Appalachian Mountains extending from southern Pennsylvania to northern Georgia. The Skyline Drive and the Blue Ridge Parkway enable the bicyclist to experience a large portion of the Blue Ridge Mountains. These two roads can transport you from Front Royal, Virginia, just 67 miles from Washington, D.C., to Cherokee, in the southwest corner of North Carolina at the gateway of Great Smoky Mountain National Park. The Skyline Drive extends 105 miles from Front Royal to Rockfish Gap just outside Waynesboro, Virginia. At Rockfish Gap the road continues uninterrupted as the Blue Ridge Parkway.

Although elevations in the Blue Ridge are modest compared to the Rockies or the Sierra Nevada, changes in elevation on the Skyline Drive and the Parkway are fairly irregular. The highest elevation on the Skyline Drive and the Blue Ridge Parkway (hereafter referred to as "the Parkway") is 6,053 feet at Richland Balsam, in the Great Balsams, between Mt. Pisgah and Cherokee. The next highest elevations either highway passes through are in the Black Mountain range which is in the southernmost section of the Parkway. One of the most exhilarating side trips off either road is the five mile climb to the summit of Mt. Mitchell which, at 6,684 feet, is the highest point

Grandfather Mountain looms ahead. Photo by Elizabeth Skinner.

in the eastern United States. The lowest point on the combined roads is near Otter Creek in Virginia, at 649 feet.

After many talks with bicyclists on the Parkway and the Skyline Drive, we think it is fair to say that changes in elevation are a major preoccupation with bicyclists who undertake the Blue Ridge. If we have learned nothing else in our thousands of miles logged on the Parkway and the Skyline Drive, it is that cycling is much more enjoyable if you can somehow manage to suspend all worry about elevation and just take it as it comes. Conceding that elevation is critical to cyclists, we have detailed changes in elevation in our point-by-point descriptive section.

The Blue Ridge Mountains have several distinct histories, all equally fascinating. The most fundamental of these histories is that of geologic time. As a part of the Appalachian Mountain range, the

Blue Ridge Mountains are among the oldest on earth. As you cycle past sheer granite walls, some blasted through in the construction of these roads, think about the amount of time Pre-Cambrian rock represents. The geologic upheaval that formed the Appalachian mountain range took place about 200 million years ago during the Paleozoic era.

For bicyclists, wind is often the dominant element dictating pace and the effort required to travel from point A to point B. Wind has had millions of years to smooth and carve the Blue Ridge. Angles along the Blue Ridge are not severe and jagged like the Rockies, but windswept and misty with mosses, wildflowers, balsam, rhododendron and mountain laurel easing mountain back to earth. Edward Abbey brings the geologic history of the Appalachians to its logical conclusion in *Appalachian Wilderness*:

> What the future holds for the mountains, according to geology, is simply a long continuation of the present erosional downgrading which will end, presumably, given enough time and if the world lasts that long, with the Appalachians as we know them reduced to a more or less featureless peneplain—to no more, that is, than a gently rolling surface of rock and field and forest (we hope) not much above sea level.

We are lucky to have these mountains here in the South. People gravitate to the timelessness and calm of the Blue Ridge for renewal and refuge. Interestingly, Great Smoky Mountain National Park happens to be the most heavily visited park in the National Park System.

A second history that began much before any talk of national parks chronicles the people who settled in the Blue Ridge. Many of these people were of Scotch-Irish descent. Another significant group was that of German immigrants from the Black Forest who introduced techniques for building cabins out of raw materials similar to those left in their homeland. All who persisted and survived the rugged conditions and isolation of the Blue Ridge surmounted many obstacles. The folklore and specialized knowledge these mountain people possessed is now celebrated as a unique and important heritage.

Opportunities for reflection on the people of the Blue Ridge are readily available along the Skyline Drive and the Parkway. The National Park Service has designed displays, signs, and visitor centers to illustrate the lifestyle of the early settlers. There are several sites that demonstrate the daily life of the mountain culture. The working farm at Humpback Rocks Visitor Center is run by Park Service staff who dress in period costume and tend the farm using early methods. The grist mill at Mabry Mill operates year-round. There is no better place than Mabry Mill to see authentic apparatus used to make sorghum, molasses, and apple butter during the fall season. Caudill Cabin, visible in the Doughton Park area, invites the traveler to speculate on the isolation of existence in the Blue Ridge.

Anyone who does even a week's bicycle tour of the Blue Ridge can experience a hint of the vulnerability early settlers experienced in this unyielding, sparsely populated area. Although the mountains are becoming increasingly developed in tourist areas, the Parkway and Skyline Drive continue to remain uncluttered by modern conveniences such as fast food and mini-malls. For those, the Blue Ridge still requires us to descend from its peaks, however narrow National Park boundaries may be.

On the other hand, the Moses H. Cone Memorial Park and Mount Pisgah provide a glimpse into the wealth of the famous industrialists, Moses H. Cone and George Vanderbilt, who built lavish mountain retreats. The contrast between subsistence farmers whose livelihood depends upon the mountains and tourists who come to the Blue Ridge for sport and leisure has always been great.

The history of the construction of the Skyline Drive and the Parkway is rife with controversy. A number of proposed routes were mapped out before the present one was settled on. The state of Tennessee campaigned heavily to host the Parkway, but ultimately lost out to North Carolina. The visionary behind a road that would connect Shenandoah National Park to Great Smoky Mountain National Park is said to have been Virginia senator Harry F. Byrd. However, Theodore E. Straus, who was a Public Works Administrator from Maryland, is also credited as the originator of the idea.

Officially, Franklin D. Roosevelt, Congress, the Virginia State legislature, the people of Virginia and North Carolina, and the National Park Service were responsible for following through with the project. The Skyline Drive was begun through an act of Congress. Due to the stipulation that no federal money be spent to acquire land for the Skyline Drive, the Virginia State Legislature appropriated over a million dollars and then solicited the people of Virginia to donate land and matching funds. The Skyline Drive was completed in 1939 by the Civilian Conservation Corps.

President Roosevelt was so pleased by the success of the Skyline Drive that he approved a joint project by the National Park Service and the Bureau of Public Roads to connect Shenandoah National Park with the Great Smoky Mountains National Park. The Blue Ridge Parkway was not officially complete until 1987 with the opening of the Linn Cove Viaduct. Before its completion travelers had to take a brief detour in the Boone-Blowing Rock area to circumvent Grandfather Mountain which is privately owned.

Although the Linn Cove Viaduct is celebrated as an engineering marvel, the entire Skyline Drive and Parkway project is masterful. It is astounding that so many diverse groups of people came together to build the mountain highway: politicians vocal with their agendas, government officials persistent in their task of overseeing the project, highway engineers and landscape architects focused on the path of the road, mountain folk employed by the Civilian Conservation Corps during the Depression, skilled artisans brought in from Europe to craft the elegant stone bridges and tunnels, landowners who were coaxed into selling their land, and naturalists concerned with the environmental impact of the road.

Since this book champions what the Parkway and Skyline Drive have to offer bicyclists, there are four simple facts that make these roads ideal for our mode of travel. There are no route changes to contend with; the road surface is well above average; commercial traffic is prohibited; and the speed limit is much lower than a regular highway.

That there are no route changes should be clear. The Skyline Drive makes a seamless transition into the Blue Ridge Parkway at Rockfish Gap, Virginia. If you are traveling north, you will be required to pay a small fee upon entering the Skyline Drive from the Parkway. The Skyline Drive is a toll road and fees are collected at all entrance stations. This entitles you to seven days of travel along the Skyline Drive.

From time to time, we have been disoriented on whether to head north or south when driving or cycling up onto the Parkway from an entrance ramp. When you enter at random from a highway that intersects the Parkway you encounter a sign that states simply: Blue Ridge Parkway (with arrows pointing north or south). You usually must commit yourself, and proceed in either direction, in order to find a sign that states a destination and its mileage. The Skyline Drive has four designated entry points. Front Royal, Virginia is the northernmost entry point followed by Thornton Gap, Swift Run Gap, and Rockfish Gap. Signage is very clear at all of these points.

The road surface on both highways is excellent. However, conditions do change with time. For example, during the 1988 season the Park Service upgraded much of the drainage system and some of the overlooks along the Skyline Drive. This meant several construction sites where traffic had to be routed onto a single lane. On the Parkway, Twin Tunnels were being repaired. The Park Service was also doing major road work between Asheville and Mt. Pisgah. These are all situations where the Park Service was in the process of maintaining and upgrading the road.

The only section on either road with a generally poor surface is between Roanoke and Rocky Knob. In this section there are frequent ruts and potholes. If you are concerned about problems with road conditions we suggest you call ahead of time for a current report on ongoing construction. For conditions along the Skyline Drive call Information at (703)999-2229; on the Parkway call the Oteen

Mileposts mark every mile along the Skyline Drive and Blue Ridge Parkway. Photo by Charlie Skinner.

District Office at (704)259-0701. You can also ask a Park Ranger upon arrival at either Park. For emergencies call 1-800-PARKWAY.

Although the Park Service actively maintains these roads, weather and erosion can create temporary problems. Fallen rocks, broken limbs or fallen trees, dead animals, and roads slick with rain or ice are potential problems. The Park Service has posted signs in falling rock zones. You will also find warning signs for deer crossings and signs announcing all tunnels.

Both roads are clearly marked with signs denoting overlooks, campgrounds, picnic areas, ranger stations, intersecting highways, elevation points, hiking trails, and any other facilities sponsored by the National Park Service. The Park Service prohibits all advertising along these roads. Some enterprising business people perch signs on hillsides beyond park boundaries, hopeful that travelers will spot them as they gaze at the countryside. In many cases, country stores and motels go unnoticed even though they are less than a mile from the road.

One sign that carries great significance for bicyclists is the milepost marker. Stone mileposts are positioned at each mile on both the Skyline Drive and the Parkway. Just as you can get hung up on elevation, anticipating every mile is no fun either. They're hard to miss, though. Most of us probably register every single marker subconsciously. Milepost markers are indispensable in charting your way through the Blue Ridge. It's not likely you will ever get lost on the Skyline Drive or the Parkway.

There is no paved shoulder or bicycle lane on either road, but we have never felt this to be a great loss. The road is amply wide enough for a car and a bike. The only vehicles that sometimes cause problems are recreational vehicles. RV's (recreational vehicles) are a problem when their drivers underestimate the size of the vehicle on the road. Also, beware of wide mirrors on pickups or vehicles towing campers. The full length of some people's camping entourage is amazing and, from a bicyclist's perspective, insane. It is common to see a full-sized pickup truck pulling an Airstream camper and a car for sightseeing—the total camping unit. As horrific as this sounds, we can deal with it when we consider that the maximum speed limit on the Skyline Drive is 35 MPH, and only 45 MPH on the Parkway. Do keep in mind that "scenic highway" implies tourist traffic. The majority of travelers on these roads are there to sightsee. Drivers are not always intent upon driving. Cars occasionally come to abrupt stops or suddenly pull off the road; erratic behavior is common.

Never having to worry about truck traffic is a major advantage the Skyline Drive and the Parkway offer bicyclists. We all cope with so many adverse conditions on unrestricted roads that not having to worry about ten tons of steel looming from behind is very liberating. Even if you are highly selective about the roads you cycle, a highway that prohibits commercial traffic is rare. You may encounter occasional delivery trucks headed for one of the Park Service concessions, but they take the most expedient route on and off these roads.

There are two primary differences between the Skyline Drive and the Blue Ridge Parkway. For one, the Skyline Drive is a private, toll road. Secondly, elevations on the Skyline Drive do not reach the extremes of those on the Parkway. The highest point on the Skyline Drive is 3,680 feet. Generally, the Skyline Drive rides a plateau. Once you have climbed up to the 3,000-foot range, you will find markedly less variation in elevation than on the Parkway until you descend at either end. By comparison, the Parkway has wild variations in elevation. For example, in a 30-mile stretch from Otter Creek to the Peaks of Otter, you cycle from the lowest point on the Parkway at 649 feet to the highest point on the Parkway in Virginia at 3,950 feet.

One other difference between the Skyline Drive and the Parkway is the number of Park concessions. The Skyline Drive has an abundance of restaurants, campgrounds, and lodges well-spaced for bicyclists. The Parkway is less consistent; Park Service concessions are as close together as 35 miles and as far apart as 70 miles. Alternatives become necessary, so you need to plan carefully.

The Park Service has put some thought into the reality of bicyclists and motorists coexisting on the Parkway and the Skyline Drive by announcing in their literature the necessity that motorists be alert to bicyclists. For example, bicycle warning signs are present at the opening of each of the 27 tunnels on the Parkway and the single tunnel on the Skyline Drive.

Visibility in these tunnels is cause for concern and should be taken seriously. None of the tunnels have artificial lighting, so the longer tunnels are pitch black inside. Even with lights we have felt out of control in some tunnels, especially those south of Waterrock Knob near Cherokee. The descent in this area ranges from 5,718 feet to 2,020 feet. Just imagine entering these tunnels from bright sunshine at speeds between 30 and 45 MPH. Suddenly you've lost the edge of the road and everything is black. You're still seeing the afterglow of the sun. Oh no, you hear something large and heavy rumbling up ahead. It's probably a RV. You're getting very unsure of yourself very fast. In the section on equipment we discuss how to prepare for tunnels.

We feel that bicyclists could command greater respect for their rights if they did their part to share the road with cars. In fact, the Park Service has published guidelines and warnings about road conditions for bicyclists:

Bicycling Regulations:
- Bicycle riders must comply with all applicable state and federal motor vehicle regulations.
- Bicycles may be ridden only on paved road surfaces and parking areas. Bicycles, including mountain bikes, may not be ridden on trails or walkways.
- The bicycle operator must exhibit a white light or reflector visible at least 500 feet to the front and a red light or reflector visible at least 200 feet to the rear during periods of low visibility, between the hours of sunset and sunrise, or while traveling through a tunnel.
- Bicycles must be ridden single file except when passing or turning left and well to the right-hand side of the road.
- Bicycle speed must be reasonable for control with regard to traffic, weather, road and light conditions.

For Safe Bicycling:
- Wear a bicycle helmet.
- Be sure your bicycle is in good operating condition. Carry a spare tube and tools for minor repairs.
- Wear high visibility clothing. It sets you apart from the scenery and makes you more visible to motorists.
- Avoid the Parkway during periods of low visibility. Fog and rain may occur unpredictably. Reschedule your trip for better weather or follow lower elevation routes until weather conditions improve.

- Exercise caution when riding through tunnels. Please be sure your bicycle is equipped with the proper lights or reflectors. There are twenty-six tunnels in North Carolina and one tunnel in Virginia.
- Temperatures vary greatly along the Parkway due to different elevations. Wear your clothing in layers if possible.
- Safe drinking water is available at all picnic areas, campgrounds, concession operations, and visitor centers. Water from streams and springs is unsafe for drinking unless you purify it.
- Make an honest evaluation of your abilities before beginning a bicycle trip on the Parkway. In some sections, you will climb as much as 1,100 feet in 3.4 miles.
- When cycling in a group, adjust your spacing to allow motor vehicles to pass safely.

Extended Trips:
- Some Parkway campgrounds and services are located too far apart for convenient cycling.
- Camping is permitted only at established campgrounds. In some areas, the U.S. Forest Service, State Parks, and private campgrounds are within easy distance of the Parkway. However, many operate on a seasonal basis.
- Food and lodging services are also available along and adjacent to the Parkway. Most operate seasonally.
- To assist in planning your trip, consult the Parkway Map and Blue Ridge Parkway Directory.
- Carry a simple first aid kit when possible.
- Please contact a Ranger before leaving a motor vehicle parked overnight on the Parkway.

We think these guidelines are very reasonable. Just remember what a privilege it is to have a road traverse the Blue Ridge. If you live for the ultimate road, this is it.

2 Weather in the Blue Ridge Mountains

Weather in the Blue Ridge Mountains has amazing, beautiful contrasts. Each season highlights different characteristics of the mountains. Bicycling in the southern Appalachians is great during much of the year, as long as you know what to expect, and prepare with the proper clothing. Weather can make or break a cycling trip in the Blue Ridge. That is true in any bicycling situation, but weather fronts move suddenly through the mountains, making weather a major consideration.

The Blue Ridge is famous for its display of fall colors. During autumn expect near bumper-to-bumper traffic. This is the biggest tourist time of the year. If you dislike competing with cars for your share of the road, we suggest you avoid weekends during peak leaf time.

Then November suddenly arrives with its wind and rain, which render the trees bare, and few care about the Blue Ridge except its true-blue aficionados. Houses hidden deep in the woods all summer are revealed. Ridges and other physical features of the mountains rise up in relief. Fall days on the Parkway can be crisp and bright or overcast with a somber, damp chill that has you preferring a cozy fire over a brisk ride.

Winter is perhaps the most difficult season for the bicyclist, but it can be thrilling to cycle in. From December through February (and sometimes into March), the Parkway may be best suited for cross-country skiing.

Winter is certainly the most brutal season. The gnarled, stunted trees are a testament to the harsh winds of winter. Snow and ice can be treacherous. The Park Service closes off some sections of the road with gates barring car traffic.

Ice is the most serious hazard. For this reason, we recommend mountain bikes in the winter months. There are steel-studded mountain bike tires for riding in snow and ice. Extended touring in the winter is not advised. Day trips are the most practical in winter. Not only is the road difficult, but open facilities are scarce between November 1 and May 1. Just make sure you plan carefully and know the weather forecast before you venture out. Selected Park Service campgrounds are winterized and open all winter.

Spring never seems to come soon enough for cyclists who have had to cope with bitter winter temperatures. This is aggravated by the reputation this season has for unpredictability. Even though it is officially spring on the calendar, the Blue Ridge may be destined for more weeks of bitter temperatures. During a recent March, we experienced a glorious weekend of cobalt blue skies when t-shirts, cycling shorts, socks and shoes were the only clothing we required. The next weekend the temperature dropped thirty degrees, but we thought we could handle it. We had balaclavas, tights, polypropelene, and wind jackets, and we were truly miserable. The wind was devastating. If you drive up from the Piedmont or other lower elevations, remember that the mountains can be at least ten degrees cooler.

Statistics demonstrate less precipitation in the spring months. Although we cyclists can do without rain, lack of rain in the spring months caused serious drought conditions in the Blue Ridge in 1987 and 1988. Planning a cycling trip on the Blue Ridge is risky in early spring. You really need to keep a close eye on the weather forecast and know what your tolerance level is. Good weather or bad, the greatest challenge for cyclists in the spring is getting back in top form and toughing out the longer ascents.

Summer is the premier cycling season. Temperatures are warm, the foliage is lush and green, and wildflowers and rhododendron provide bright contrasts in color. When summer finally comes it is

It's raining. Charlie stops at an overlook to lubricate his chain. Photo by Elizabeth Skinner.

With thunder clouds building, it's time to find shelter. Photo by Charlie Skinner.

a great feeling to shed all of those winter layers and cycle unencumbered by weight and bulk.

Summer in the Blue Ridge can be hot and humid; it can also be wet with sudden thunderstorms and fog. According to National Climatic Data Center statistics, the summer months are the foggiest of the year. In June, July, and August eleven is the average number of days each month with less than a quarter-mile visibility due to heavy fog. August ranks highest with an average of fourteen days of heavy fog; September comes in second with twelve days. Fog really can force you off of the Parkway and the Skyline Drive. We always tour with a flashing belt beacon for the rear of our bikes and a white light for the front. Visibility can be practically nil. Rain and fog are definite show stoppers. The odds of encountering at least one morning or afternoon of inclement weather in a week's trip are high.

To illustrate the frustrations weather can cause cyclists, we would like to talk about September. We chose September twice in the past four years for extended cycling trips. One reason why we chose September was that, statistically, it does not rank among the rainiest months in the Blue Ridge. The mean number of days with one-tenths of an inch or more of precipitation is eight. Eight to thirty, those odds don't sound too bad. Well, the first time we toured the entire length of the Skyline Drive and the Parkway, we experienced rain and fog every day for two weeks, from Front Royal, Virginia to Blowing Rock, North Carolina. On our second September tour, the last thirty-six hours were a total rainout. The moral of the story is: weather in the Blue Ridge is unpredictable, so prepare for its downside. If you cannot handle cycling through rain, you will definitely need to factor in a few extra days into your travel itinerary.

One final aspect of the weather that you should be aware of is wind. Head winds are never much of a problem in the mountains. The surprise for those who have never cycled in the mountains is wind gusting through gaps. In his *Blue Ridge Parkway Guide*, William G. Lord calls upon mountain folklore to define a "gap."

"See the outline of that mountain over thar? Them low dips in it's what's knowed as a gap. Some of 'm is whar a road or trail is located acrost the mountains." In general, the Parkway travels the crest line of the Blue Ridge and several other ranges. Therefore, it passes through a long series of gaps and intersects many cross-mountain roads.

On a windy day, gusts of wind may blow through these "gaps" in a mountain. You can be shooting down the side of a mountain only to find yourself fighting for control of your bike on the road. Most gaps are labeled by signs along the Skyline Drive and the Parkway. A firm grip on the handlebars and confident bike handling skills should prevent any mishaps.

In the final space of this chapter we have compiled data on

Low Notch Gap at the crest of the Blue Ridge—beware the occasional gust of wind. Photo by Elizabeth Skinner.

temperature and precipitation available from the National Climatic Data Center in Asheville, North Carolina.

Average Daily Maximum and Minimum Temperatures (F°)

	Jan.	Feb.	Mar.	Apr.	May.	June	July	Aug.	Sept.	Oct.	Nov.	Dec.
Asheville	47	51	58	69	76	81	84	83	78	69	59	50
	26	28	34	43	51	58	62	62	56	43	34	28
Boone	44	46	52	62	71	77	79	79	73	65	53	44
	25	25	31	38	47	55	59	58	51	41	32	25
Roanoke	45	48	57	68	76	83	87	85	79	69	57	48
	26	28	35	44	53	60	65	64	57	45	36	29
Peaks of Otter	n/a	n/a	n/a	64	72	77	81	79	73	63	n/a	n/a
			43	52	58	63	62	56	46			
Big Meadows	n/a	n/a	n/a	59	67	74	76	75	69	60	n/a	n/a
			37	46	54	57	56	50	41			

Average Monthly Precipitation in Inches

	Jan.	Feb.	Mar.	Apr.	May	June	July	Aug.	Sept.	Oct.	Nov.	Dec.
Asheville	3.48	3.60	5.13	3.84	4.19	4.20	4.43	4.79	3.96	3.29	3.29	3.51
Boone	4.05	4.08	5.14	4.45	4.34	4.52	5.94	5.33	4.40	3.16	4.34	3.94
Roanoke	2.83	3.19	3.69	3.09	3.51	3.34	3.45	3.91	3.14	3.48	2.59	2.93
Peaks of Otter	n/a	n/a	n/a	n/a	n/a	n/a	n/a	5.50	n/a	3.51	n/a	n/a
Big Meadows	n/a	n/a	n/a	3.63	n/a	n/a	n/a	5.47	n/a	n/a	n/a	n/a

* Data not available for Peaks of Otter and Big Meadows.

Mean Number of Days With .01 Inches or More of Precipitation

	Jan.	Feb.	Mar.	Apr.	May	June	July	Aug.	Sep.	Oct.	Nov.	Dec.
Asheville	10	9	11	9	12	11	12	12	9	8	9	10
Boone (.10 inch or more)	9	7	9	8	8	9	11	9	7	5	6	7
Roanoke	10	10	11	10	12	10	12	11	8	8	9	9

3 Camping vs. Lodging

If you are considering an extended tour of the Skyline Drive and the Parkway, the first decision you will probably make is whether to camp or stay in motels. There are pros and cons to both approaches. However, if you can afford motels, your trip will be easier and possibly more comfortable. Without sleeping bag, pad, tent, and cooking gear you can make better time on the road. Credit card touring is definitely the streamlined, light way to go.

Many lodges along the Skyline Drive and Parkway are memorable with their high ceilings and exposed beams, large stone fireplaces, decks and porches for lounging, and restaurants featuring southern mountain cooking. From people-watching by the fireplace in the great room at Big Meadows to gazing out at cow pastures on the deck at Bluffs Lodge, they all heighten the rustic mountain experience.

There are five lodges within strict Park Service boundaries of the Skyline Drive and the Parkway. Although Skyland Lodge and Big Meadows Lodge are well-spaced lodges along the Skyline Drive, the lodges along the Parkway are far apart. Peaks of Otter Lodge is 150 miles from Bluffs Lodge at Doughton Park. After that, the only other Park Service lodge is at Mt. Pisgah. In Part Two of the book we outline all Park Service and private facilities along these roads.

All of the restaurants and lodges along the Skyline Drive and the Parkway are run by private concessioners. There are no other businesses within the boundaries of either Park. Essentially, the Blue Ridge Parkway boundaries are very small as the road winds through the Blue Ridge. The major facilities along the Parkway include: Otter Creek, Peaks of Otter, Roanoke Mountain, Rocky

Knob, Mabry Mill, Cumberland Knob, Doughton Park, Moses H. Cone, Julian Price Memorial Park, Linville Falls, Crabtree Meadows, Craggy Gardens, and Mt. Pisgah. The Skyline Drive differs because it is surrounded by the much larger Shenandoah National Park. While the Park Service maintains facilities at Matthews Arm, Skyland, Big Meadows, Lewis Mountain, and Loft Mountain, the surrounding areas along the Skyline Drive are protected as national forest lands.

Because the Parkway has so few facilities within its boundaries in proportion to its length, we have provided you with information on motels and campgrounds off of the Parkway. When you study the Parkway map you see that it is feasible to tour from Park Service campground to campground. There are some long, difficult stretches between these campgrounds. It is 70 miles from Rocky Knob campground to Doughton Park campground; 65 miles from Doughton Park to the next Park Service campground at Julian Price. That may be more than you want to cover in a day. And if it rains or fog sets in, what then? That's why you need alternatives when touring the Parkway. Things hardly ever turn out the way you planned.

Park Service campgrounds are distinctive in several ways. They are all situated within large tracts of Park Service land ranging in size from 250 acres to 7,000 acres. Most of these campgrounds are fairly secluded in wooded areas. Like the lodges, each campground has a charm all its own. Otter Creek has its namesake flowing alongside campsites; Peaks of Otter and Julian Price are situated beside lakes; deer roam freely throughout Big Meadows; and you pitch your tent amidst gnarled, ancient balsams at Mt. Pisgah. Big Meadows on the Skyline Drive is the largest campground with 227 sites. The smallest, Lewis Mountain Campground, is also on the Skyline Drive. It has 31 sites.

The big difference between Skyline Drive and Parkway campgrounds is that Skyline Drive campgrounds all have pay showers. There are absolutely no showers in Blue Ridge Parkway campgrounds. Shenandoah National Park (Skyline Drive) caters to visitors with more conveniences than the Parkway. The campstores are much more elaborate. The campgrounds along the Skyline Drive also have laundry facilities. Although there are several private campgrounds along the Parkway with shower and laundry facilities, none of the Park Service campgrounds on the Parkway have either convenience. Most likely, backpackers on the Appalachian Trail are the reason for these amenities on the Skyline Drive. With the Appalachian Trail running through Shenandoah National Park and paralleling the Skyline Drive, Park Service facilities are the primary source for hikers. The Appalachian Trail intersects the Parkway at a few points, but these are not near Park Service facilities.

The physical layout of the typical campground in both Parks is very similar. Paved roads run through the campgrounds. There are separate areas for tent and recreational vehicles. Each site has a groomed tent pad, picnic table, and grill. Within clustered sites you will find running water, bathrooms, and trash receptacles. Some campgrounds have bear poles if the campground is located in "bear country." All campgrounds have an amphitheater or another gathering place, pay telephones, and rangers on duty.

Rates for Skyline Drive campgrounds are $8.00/site ($10.00/site at Big Meadows). The Parkway charges $8.00/site in all campgrounds. All campgrounds are filled on a first-come, first-served basis except Big Meadows, which utilizes the Mistix reservation system. Call 1-800-365-CAMP to place a reservation.

We think camping is a great experience in and of itself. Although it does require more effort in the long run, combining camping with lodging allows you the best of both worlds. A fully loaded touring bike gives you all the options. If you decide you can go no further, but there is nothing civilized for miles, you can pull off the road and have a tent over your head and the means to cook a decent meal. With credit card touring you must plan ahead. If you are not capable of covering the mileage to make your motel reservation there is little to fall back on.

The best way to decide which approach to bicycle touring suits you is to weigh the pros and cons. We figure it can't hurt to spell them all out.

Advantages of Camping:
- Camping is less expensive.
- Camping is an experience in and of itself.
- There is a tendency to meet more people. Campers seem to open up to the novelty of the touring cyclist.
- You have more options. With facilities sometimes far apart, it is a plus to have both camping and lodging possibilities.

Disadvantages of Camping:
- The extra gear required increases the weight you must carry.
- Housekeeping chores, such as setting up and breaking camp, require more time.
- There are no showers in Parkway campgrounds.
- You must be prepared for inclement weather.
- During peak times, some campgrounds fill up. The campgrounds on the Skyline Drive reach capacity more often than those on the Parkway. If camping at Big Meadows on the Skyline Drive make sure you make reservations ahead of time (through Ticketron). It can be impossible to obtain sites on holidays and other peak times.
- Only a few selected Park Service campgrounds are open in the winter months.

Advantages of Lodging:
- Spending your nights in motels allows streamlined, efficient touring: no sleeping bags, tents, cooking gear, etc.
- With less weight you can tour faster and cover more miles each day.
- There are some wonderful lodges along the Skyline Drive and the Parkway.
- You can expect the creature comforts of home: showers, a warm, dry bed, TV, etc.

Disadvantages of Lodging:

- Reservations are advisable and, at peak times, required.
- Most motels have required check in times. If you fail to arrive at your destination on time you may lose your room. Usually, you can guarantee a room with a major credit card.
- Motels and lodges are open seasonally. Generally, this is May 1 through October 31.
- Rates are subject to change.

4   Gearing Up: Special Equipment and Clothing

When making choices on equipment and clothing for bicycling in the mountains, three tenets should be foremost in your mind:
- know your abilities
- know your bicycle
- anticipate the weather

Everything we say here may seem obvious, but we want to emphasize the key issues.

Bicycles and Tools

In today's high tech world, bicycles are no exception. With so much great equipment on the market, we suggest that you select the best you can afford. If you cannot purchase everything you need all at once, upgrade later. We highly recommend using sealed components as much as possible: sealed headsets bottom brackets, hubs, and pedals. In the long run, sealed components will endure, especially through adverse weather conditions.

While we choose not to discuss gear ratios, we advise you to make an honest assessment of your abilities when setting your bike up for mountain cycling. The Assault on Mt. Mitchell is an extreme case, but it is a classic example of bicyclists getting in over their heads. Each year that we participate in this 102-mile endurance event we see a steady procession of cyclists reduced to walking their bikes along the Parkway and the five miles up to the summit of Mt. Mitchell. This is not the sad fate of one or two cyclists; what you see is thirty or forty people who thought they would be able to cycle through exhaustion with the gearing they had selected. For more information on the Assault on Mt. Mitchell see the descriptive section under Mt. Mitchell.

If you are considering an extended trip of the Parkway and the Skyline Drive, and you have never toured in mountainous terrain, a triple crank set is a must. Fully loaded panniers make a difference in any terrain. Mountains truly magnify any weight you choose to carry. We have toured thousands of miles with conventional shifting mechanisms which work quite well. However, index shifting systems are ideal for mountain cycling.

Having the right tool for the right emergency is not always possible. You should carry the bare essentials on every ride. There are so few bike shops along the Skyline Drive and the Parkway that you really need to put some thought into tool selection. If you are day-tripping, it is a good idea to have at least a comprehensive selection of tools in your car and a basic tool kit on your bike. If you are making an extended tour, you want to strike a balance. The weight of tools can really add up. However, a bike emergency can leave you stranded. In some situations you may have to hitch a ride to the nearest bike shop. See Appendix A for a list of all the bike shops within a reasonable distance of the Parkway.

If you need help selecting tools and equipment for your bike, we suggest you take your bike to your local bike shop and ask a mechanic for advice. All good bike shops are more than happy to spend time showing you how to use the proper tools to make minor adjustments on your bike. Of course, any time you cycle on the Parkway you should make sure your bike is in top condition.

One investment you might consider is quality wheels. Hand-built wheels with sealed hubs should spare you much aggravation. In any event, two tools you will want on hand if you are touring are a spoke wrench and spare spokes.

We have compiled a list of the tools we think are absolutely essential. Most of these tools will fit in the type of bag that mounts under a bicycle saddle. If you are making day trips you can leave off the spokes, cables, and spare tire.

Charlie's List of Essential Tools
  chain breaker
  spoke wrench
  spare spokes
  pliers
  small adjustable wrench
  allen wrenches
  tire levers
  brake cable(front & rear)
  derailleur cable(front & rear)
  spare tire, tubes & patch kit
  multi-purpose lubricant
  air pump(which attaches to bike frame)

Make sure your air pump works properly and has the correct head for the type of tube you use, Presta® or Schrader®. Just remember, on the Parkway and the Skyline Drive proper there is practically zero availability of bicycle parts. A rudimentary knowledge of bicycle repair is a required bicycle skill.

If you have absolutely no mechanical aptitude you might want to carry a small repair manual that can guide you through basic repairs. We recommend one of the following titles:

The Bike Bag Book by Tom Cuthbertson and Rick Morrall,
    Ten Speed Press, 1981.

Roadside Bicycle Repairs: The Simple Guide to Fixing Your Bike
    by Rob Van der Plas, Bicycle Books, 1987.

After all, compared to most machines, a bicycle is not that complicated.

Clothing

Certain clothing items are essential, even for weekend trips in the Blue Ridge. Needless to say, weather should govern all the clothing choices you make. We highly recommend a Goretex® rainsuit. In our opinion, this item, above all others, is the most essential for cycling in the Blue Ridge. At the very minimum, a wind breaker or some water repellent jacket is a must. This is necessary not only for rain, but for sudden cold temperatures and windy conditions as well.

Is Goretex® fabric really worth it? We think so. We cycled in the rain with regular nylon rainsuits for years and got by. As you may know, Goretex® is great because it breathes. It does an excellent job of keeping water out, yet when your body heats up you perspire less because air is able to circulate underneath the fabric. Goretex® is not perfect, but it is a vast improvement over other fabrics.

You might think that in the summer months you won't need a rainsuit or jacket. Our experience has shown us otherwise. We have been caught in downpours on the Parkway with no choice but to will away the chill from a body-drenching rain. If nothing else, a rainsuit or jacket will help keep you warm.

In spring and fall, the temperature can fluctuate quite a bit. Chilly temperatures make tights or leg warmers a good idea. A polypropelene or Thermax® top is a good item to have on hand, even in the summer, for sudden drops in temperature. You should keep in mind that the mountains can be chilly even at the height of summer. Other than these few specifics, let personal taste dictate your choices.

One common mistake for touring cyclists is to pack too much stuff. You may not need as much clothing as you think. If laundry facilities are available along your way, you may be able to get by with less.

Ziploc® Bags

While we're on the subject of packing gear, we would like to sing the praises of one magic item, Ziploc® bags. This simple household item is indispensable for keeping your gear dry. Panniers, and other bicycle bags, are not entirely waterproof. In a downpour, Ziploc® bags will save you from a soggy mess. They also force you to pack more scientifically, since even the gallon-sized bags will only hold so much.

Helmets

It is a grave mistake not to wear a helmet when bicycling. There is no valid reason for not wearing one. We sincerely urge you to wear a helmet at all times while cycling and to wear it properly—not cocked back away from your forehead or unfastened.

Lighting systems

Due to the frequency of rain, fog, and tunnels on these highways, some type of lighting system is required by the Park Service. Front and rear lights could save your life. Not only do lighting systems make you more visible to cars in inclement weather, they help you find your way through the longer tunnels. Some of the tunnels you will encounter are long enough, or curved enough, to leave you in total darkness. Not only can cars inflict injury, you can easily do damage to yourself by taking a spill on a rock or running into the wall of a tunnel.

We use a flashing belt beacon for the rear of our bikes and a white light for the front. Generator and battery operated lights each have advantages. Extra bulbs and batteries are a good idea. Some of the smaller bike shops do not stock a specific item like bulbs for belt beacons.

The Checklist

Finally, we provide you with a master list of the things you should think about taking for the long haul. If you are going out on weekend trips, you can obviously cut things out. We have learned the hard way about carrying too much gear on a bicycle. In 1985, we cycled halfway across the country before we learned how to pack efficiently. To our relief, we finally had it right when we toured the Skyline Drive. We cycled from Front Royal to Asheville without a wobble. If you can get by with less, do it.

What To Bring For An Extended Tour Of The Blue Ridge

cycling shorts, 2 pairs
T-shirts or cycling jerseys, 3
polypropelene or Thermax®
   top, 1
running shorts, 1 pair
shorts, 1 pair
Goretex® rainsuit
lightweight wind jacket
swimsuit
socks, underwear, etc.
cycling gloves
cycling hat, optional
cycling helmet, highly
   recommended
cycling shoes
shoes, alternate pair
sandals or flipflops, optional

towel, 1 (as lightweight as
   you can find)
toiletries
first aid kit
wristwatch
sunglasses
sunscreen
camera & film
notepad, pens, stamps, etc.
flashlight, small
cookstove, fuel, & matches
mess kit (don't forget the
   can opener)
rope (a multi-purpose item)
lightweight sleeping bag
   & pad
tent & ground cloth

Part 2:
Point-by-Point
Descriptions

In our point-by-point breakdown of the Skyline Drive and the Parkway we list motels, lodges, restaurants, grocery stores, and campgrounds on and off of these roads. We also list area hospitals and any bicycle shops within a reasonable distance. Bicycle shops are not in abundance. Because of this, we also list hardware stores that might help you out of a jam.

Our criteria for including facilities off of these roads take several factors into account. We have not ventured more than five miles off these roads with the exception of a few towns we choose to highlight. In most cases, we have not included facilities more than one to three miles off the road. We have investigated all side roads except those that are strictly residential. We do not recommend roads that involve extreme descents unless there is something on that road to justify an arduous climb back up.

We have not rated the quality of facilities, although we do make remarks about those that made a favorable impression upon us.

Blue Ridge Parkway campgrounds are $8.00 per campsite per night. Skyline Drive campgrounds are $8.00 per campsite per night (Big Meadows is $10.00 per campsite per night).

We have devised a rating system for the cost of motels and lodges. These rates are subject to change.

$	inexpensive	up to $35.00
$$	moderate	$36.00-$55.00
$$$	expensive	$56.00+

We begin at Milepost 0 on the Skyline Drive and travel south. If you decide to travel north just work backwards from specific mileposts. Generally, we divide our sections by Park Service facilities. In some cases, a town will be the dividing point.

There are as many approaches to bicycling in the Blue Ridge as there are riders. A strong rider with gear could reasonably tour the Skyline Drive in two days. Unencumbered by gear, one could cycle the Skyline Drive in a single day. Then again, there are so many things to see along the way, and so many trails to hike, that spending a week there would not be unreasonable.

5 The Skyline Drive

The Skyline Drive is a scenic highway that runs the length of Shenandoah National Park for a total of 105 miles. Shenandoah National Park (hereafter referred to as "the Park") is comprised of 195,000 acres of the George Washington National Forest located in western Virginia. Not only is there a scenic highway dissecting the Park, but 95 miles of the Appalachian Trail are within Park boundaries. As you cycle along the Skyline Drive, the Shenandoah Valley runs parallel to the west while the Piedmont extends eastward toward the coast.

Small details in the construction of the Skyline Drive give it a slightly different atmosphere from the Blue Ridge Parkway. Stone and mortar walls grace the edge of the road as it winds along the Blue Ridge Mountains. These structures and the tendency of the trees to form a canopy over the road, give the Drive a secluded feeling.

Since the Skyline Drive runs continuously through national forest land, wildlife may be more prevalent here than along the Parkway. There is a large Virginia white-tailed deer population in Shenandoah National Park. You are guaranteed to spot deer at dawn or dusk. Black bear also inhabit the Park. Although bear sightings are uncommon, Matthews Arm and Loft Mountain campgrounds have bearproof trash cans and bear poles for hoisting food. A bear census taken by the National Park Service and the Virginia State Wildlife Commission estimates the bear population to be around 300 during the summer. Other wildlife include the red fox, gray fox, striped skunk, spotted skunk, bobcat, racoon, beaver, groundhog, and chipmunk. There are about 200 species of birds in the Park. Among the larger birds in the Park you will find the wild turkey, the raven, and the ruffled grouse.

The trees that make up the George Washington National Forest are primarily young second growth as a result of heavy timbering practiced before the Park was established. The primary species are oak and hickory. You will also find black locust, hemlock, yellow birch, black birch, basswood, tulip poplar, red maple, and sugar maple.

If bicycle touring in the mountains is a new experience for you, the Skyline Drive is a good place to start. Facilities abound with the largest gap between a source of food being 25 miles. There are two lodges, six restaurants, four camp stores, and four campgrounds all in the space of 105 miles. In addition, all but one of the campgrounds have showers. That is pretty good, especially when compared to those along the Parkway.

With basic needs provided for, you are free to concentrate on some very pleasant bicycling. The grades on the Skyline Drive are not as severe as they are on the Parkway. The longest climbs are at either entrance. The elevation drops to 1390 feet at the Front Royal entrance and 1900 feet at the Rockfish Gap entrance near Waynesboro.

Front Royal to Matthews Arm

Front Royal, Virginia is one of the most popular starting points for extended tours of the Blue Ridge. The closest airports to Front Royal are approximately 70 miles away in Washington, D.C. You can cycle out of either Dulles International Airport or Washington National Airport to Front Royal.

When you enter Shenandoah National Park on a bicycle, you experience the sensation of being transported into a separate world. At the height of the summer the vegetation is thick and alive with secrets, as if you were traveling through an enchanted forest. The deeper in you go the more entranced you become. Kudzu climbs greedily in the lower elevations. On hot days there is steamy humidity. Slowly, you climb from Front Royal to the higher elevations.

The fact is, you have to do some work to reach the Blue Ridge proper. The first ten miles of the Skyline Drive climb Dickey Ridge before connecting with the Blue Ridge mountain range at Compton Gap (Milepost 10.4). You climb 2,000 feet in this 22-mile stretch up to 3,385 feet at Hogback Overlook.

There are numerous overlooks in this section. At most of these overlooks the Shenandoah River is visible. Take note of the Massanutten ridge which divides the Shenandoah Valley for nearly fifty miles. When you study the rock along the Skyline Drive you are looking at molten lava flows called the Catoctin formation.

Matthews Arm is the first campground on the Skyline Drive as you travel south. There is no food here, but Elkwallow Wayside is just 2 miles south with a restaurant and camp store. There are three hikes which originate from the campground: Traces Trail, Knob Mountain, and Overall Run Falls.

Milepost

0   **Front Royal, Virginia** (elev. 590 ft.)
           Front Royal is situated at the north entrance of the

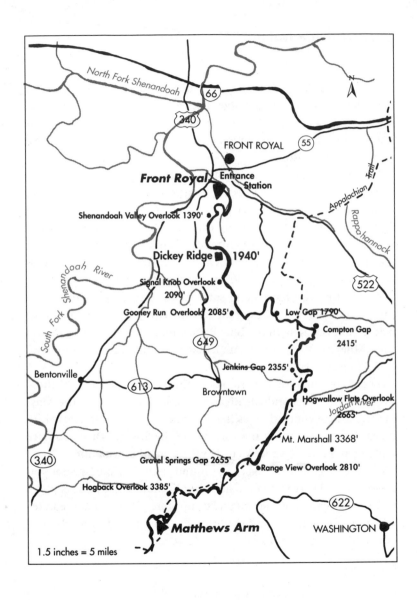

Skyline Drive. Facilities include a post office, hospital, numerous restaurants, motels, and a bicycle shop.

Constant Spring Inn (703)635-7010 $$
Located 3 blocks from the Skyline Drive at U.S. 340 and U.S. 55.

Front Royal Motel (703)635-4114 $–$$
Go 2 miles south on U.S. 522.

Pioneer Motel (703)635-4784 $$
This motel is just l block from the Skyline Drive on U.S. 340 and U.S. 55.

Shenandoah Motel (703)635-3181 $
Located 2.5 miles north on U.S. 340.

Mike's Bike & Hobby Shop (703)635-5864
Located in the Royal Plaza Shopping Center just a quarter mile from the Skyline Drive.
Hours: Monday-Saturday 10 A.M.–5 P.M.

4.6   **Dickey Ridge Visitor Center** (elev. 1,940 ft.)
The information center has a ranger on duty to answer questions. This facility includes exhibits, publications sales, water, restrooms, a picnic area, and a nature trail. There is no camping or food here.

21   **Hogback Overlook** (elev. 3,385 ft.)
This is the highest point so far. Hogback Overlook affords excellent views of the Shenandoah Valley and Shenandoah River.

22.2   **Matthews Arm** (elev. 2,750 ft.)
This is the most primitive campground on the Skyline Drive. There are no showers or laundry facilities here. If you need supplies, the Elkwallow Wayside is 2 miles south with a restaurant and camp store. There are 186 campsites here.

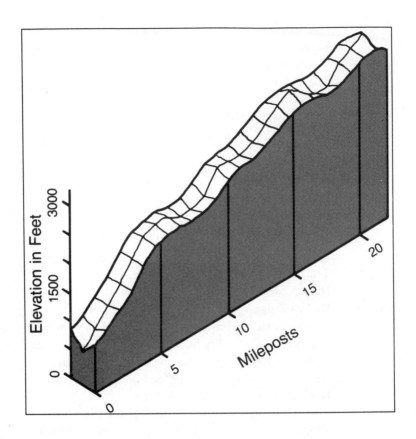

Matthews Arm to Skyland

In this 20-mile stretch you dip down to 2,304 feet at the Thornton Gap Entrance Station and then climb to the highest point on the Skyline Drive, 3,680 feet, just before the entrance to the Skyland Lodge.

The numerous hiking trails that highlight streams, waterfalls, and geologic formations are good reasons for taking your time along the Skyline Drive. The trail to Jeremy's Run, one of the major trout streams in the Park, originates at Elkwallow Picnic Area. At Thornton Gap you can view Marys Rock, which is formed of granodiorite. Marys Rock Tunnel, just south of Thornton Gap, is the only tunnel on the Skyline Drive. As you make your way toward Skyland Lodge, views of Pinnacles and the profile of Stony Man Mountain dominate the area.

Skyland is one of two lodges along the Drive. If you're not spending the night at Skyland, consider having lunch here. The dining rooms at Skyland's and the Panorama Restaurant are filled with windows perfect for gazing at the Shenandoah Valley.

Milepost

24   **Elkwallow Wayside and Picnic Area**
        There's a restaurant and a campstore here.

31.5   **Panorama Restaurant**
        At Thornton Gap, this restaurant would make a good
        lunch stop. You can view Marys Rocks from the deck.

36.7   **Pinnacles**
        Pinnacles is a picnic area and a point of access to the
        Appalachian Trail.

41.7   **Skyland Lodge** (703)999-2211 $$–$$$
        Skyland has a lodge, restaurant, tap room, and gift
        shop. There is no camping here.

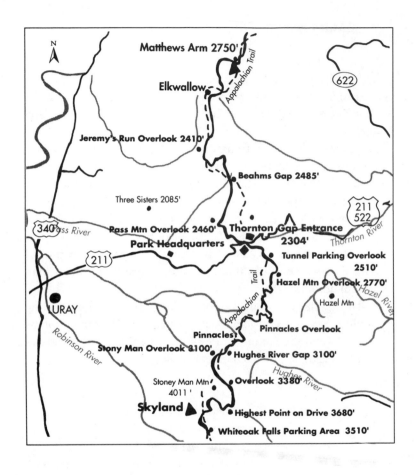

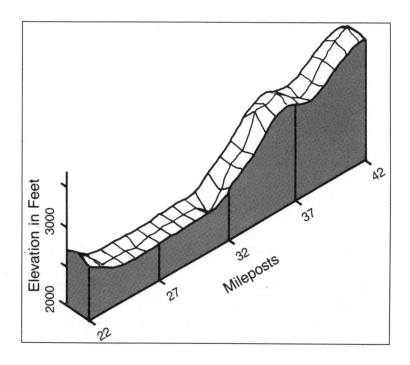

Skyland to Big Meadows

This brief 10-mile stretch has much scenic beauty with Hawksbill Mountain dominating as the highest peak in Shenandoah National Park at 4,051 feet. The Franklin Cliffs Overlook between Mileposts 49 and 50 has great rocky cliffs perfect for a siesta on a sunny day. If you have time for an hour's hike, Dark Hollow Falls is a good choice at Milepost 50.7, just north of Big Meadows.

When we think of Big Meadows, two things immediately come to mind: blueberries and deer. Deer sightings are possible at all times of day. At dawn and dusk, the meadow directly across from the Visitor Center attracts anywhere from ten to fifty grazing deer. Take note that the meadow is filled with blueberries ripe for picking in July and August.

Big Meadows is the most extensive facility on the Skyline Drive. The campground here uses the Ticketron reservation system. Without a reservation, camping is out of the question at peak times. Big Meadows Lodge has a cozy, rustic charm. We spent two memorable days fogged and rained in here one September. The dining room and great room of the lodge have high ceilings with exposed beams and wrought iron ceiling fixtures. The massive stone fireplace in the great room has magnetic force on foul-weather days.

Big Meadows is a major stop for hikers on the Appalachian Trail. The camp store here is superbly stocked. Food items have been selected in sizes and types suitable for campers. The camp store sells clothing and supplies, such as candles, Coleman fuel, parkas, jeans, and toiletries. Big Meadows is the halfway point on the Skyline Drive. As we said earlier, a strong rider could cover the Skyline Drive in two days with Big Meadows being the logical overnight stop.

Milepost

46.7   **Upper Hawksbill Parking Area**
Hawksbill Mountain is the highest point in the park at

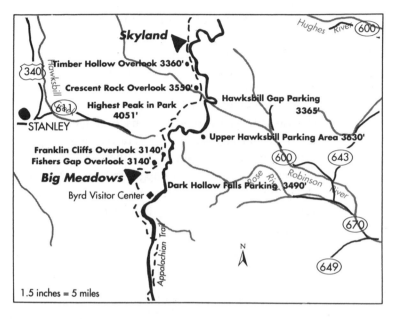

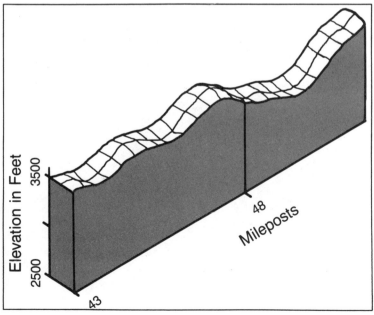

4,051 feet. The trail to the summit is 2 miles round trip.

50.7   **Dark Hollow Falls**

The trail to the falls is 1.5 miles round trip.

51   **Big Meadows**

Big Meadows Lodge (703)999-2221 $$–$$$

This rustic lodge has rooms, cabins, dining facilities, a tap room, and a gift shop. Big Meadows has a campground with showers, laundry facilities, and an excellent camp store. The campground has 227 sites. The visitors center conducts a variety of naturalist's programs each day. The number for reservations is 1-800-365-CAMP.

Big Meadows to Lewis Mountain

If you plan on camping at the halfway point on the Skyline Drive, Lewis Mountain is a good alternative to Big Meadows. Lewis Mountain campground has fewer campsites, but the atmosphere is less hectic, without the constant flow of traffic the Big Meadows complex attracts. There are also a few housekeeping cabins here which require a reservation.

The elevation in this section remains fairly constant in the 3,000 to 3,500-foot range. Be on the lookout for deer.

A hike to Bearfence Mountain summit is great if you have the time. It is only an eight-tenths of a mile hike round-trip for a 360-degree view of the area. From this rocky summit you can see Massanutten Ridge, Shenandoah Valley, Grindstone, Green, Powell, and Smith Mountains to the west. To the east, there are a dozen peaks within view—Hazeltop, Bush Mountain, Laurel Gap, and Buzzard Rocks are among them. Henry Heatwole's book, *Guide To Skyline Drive and Shenandoah National Park*, actually includes sketches identifying the geologic features at each overlook along the Skyline Drive. At Milepost 56.4, this hike is only a mile from Lewis Mountain. You might want to drop your gear, set up camp, and cycle back for a hike.

Milepost

56.4   **Bearfence Mountain Parking Area**
        The hike to the summit is only eight-tenths of a mile round-trip.

57.5   **Lewis Mountain** (703)999-2255 $$ (Cabins)
        You will find complete facilities here including a campground, housekeeping cabins, showers, laundry facilities, and a well-stocked camp store. This camp store has food and camping equipment on half the scale of the Big Meadows store. Lewis Mountain has 31 campsites.

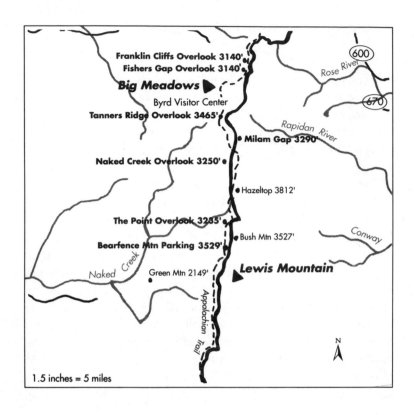

Franklin Cliffs Overlook 3140'
Fishers Gap Overlook 3140'
Big Meadows
Byrd Visitor Center
Tanners Ridge Overlook 3465'

Milam Gap 3290'

Naked Creek Overlook 3250'

Hazeltop 3812'

Rose River

Rapidan River

The Point Overlook 3235'

Bush Mtn 3527'

Bearfence Mtn Parking 3529'

Conway

Naked Creek

Green Mtn 2149'

Lewis Mountain

Appalachian Trail

600

670

N

1.5 inches = 5 miles

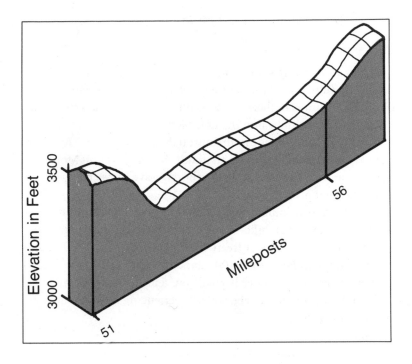

Lewis Mountain to Loft Mountain

If you are heading south you have a great 1,000-foot descent to Swift Run Gap, one of four entrance stations on the Skyline Drive. From Swift Run Gap there is a mixed bag of up and down, but the road ultimately climbs into the Loft Mountain area.

Loft Mountain Wayside is directly off the Skyline Drive. However, the road to the campground is an uphill challenge. If Loft Mountain campground is your destination for the day, save some energy for the climb to the top.

Loft Mountain campground has some outstanding campsites. It is worth dragging your bike down into one of the more secluded wooded sites. Deer wander freely through these areas. The Appalachian Trail is no more than 100 yards from one side of the campground; it's great to have just beyond your tent. You can hike a stretch and ponder the differences between experiencing the Blue Ridge by foot and by bicycle.

Milepost

79.5   **Loft Mountain Wayside**
This restaurant serves hamburgers and other fast fare.
Loft Mountain Campground
There is a steep, 1-mile climb to the campground. Although Loft Mountain Wayside serves food, no grocery items are found there. For grocery items and camping equipment, there is a good camp store adjoining the campground. Showers, laundry facilities, and a well-stocked camp store make this a good stop for those of you doing extended tours. If you're heading south, this is your last chance for shower and laundry facilities in a Park Service campground. Loft Mountain has 221 campsites.

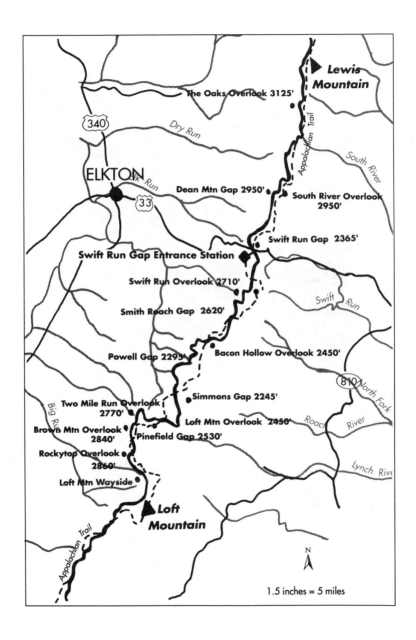

The Oaks Overlook 3125'

Lewis Mountain

340

Dry Run

Appalachian Trail

South River

ELKTON

Dean Mtn Gap 2950'

South River Overlook 2950'

33

Swift Run Gap 2365'

Swift Run Gap Entrance Station

Swift Run Overlook 2710'

Swift Run

Smith Roach Gap 2620'

Powell Gap 2295'

Bacon Hollow Overlook 2450'

810

North Fork

Simmons Gap 2245'

Two Mile Run Overlook 2770'

Loft Mtn Overlook 2450'

Roach River

Brown Mtn Overlook 2840'

Pinefield Gap 2530'

Big Run

Rockytop Overlook 2860'

Loft Mtn Wayside

Lynch River

Loft Mountain

Appalachian Trail

N

1.5 inches = 5 miles

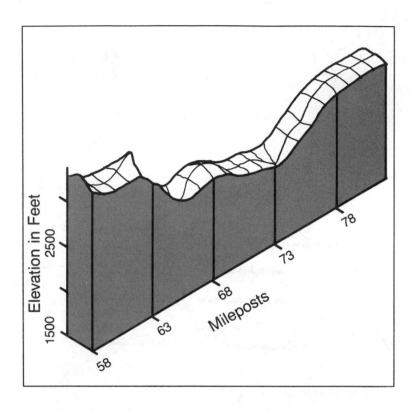

Loft Mountain to Rockfish Gap

It is 25 miles to the end of the Skyline Drive and the beginning of the Blue Ridge Parkway. If you are heading south, you have an easy descent into Rockfish Gap. If you are heading north toward Loft Mountain, you can expect a steady climb much of the way.

For travelers doing a long-distance tour of the Skyline Drive and the Parkway, Waynesboro is a good overnight stop. With a bicycle shop, medical facilities, and the full range of shopping opportunities, Waynesboro is one of the few cities in close proximity to the Skyline Drive and the Parkway. Waynesboro is situated 4 miles outside of Rockfish Gap. The only disadvantage of a stopover in Waynesboro is that you will start out with a 4-mile climb from the town proper back up to the Skyline Drive. Fortunately, if lodging and food are all you require, there are two motels just off the Skyline Drive at Rockfish Gap.

Milepost

105.4   **Rockfish Gap** (elev. 1,909 ft.)
          Rockfish Gap marks the end of the Skyline Drive.
          With little fanfare the road becomes the Blue Ridge
          Parkway. Exit here for Waynesboro. Take Highway
          250 West 4 miles into Waynesboro. Waynesboro has a
          post office, hospital, restaurants, motels and a bicycle
          shop. There are two motels at Rockfish Gap which
          could spare you the descent into town.
          Holiday Inn (703)942-5201 $$–$$$
          Proceed just off the Skyline Drive at Waynesboro exit.
          Skyline-Parkway Motor Court (703)942-9878 $$
          You will find this motel just off the Skyline Drive at
          the Waynesboro exit.
          Comfort Inn (703)942-1171 $$
          Four miles west of the Skyline Drive in Waynesboro.

The General Wayne Inn Restaurant next door has wonderful food.

Red Carpet Inn (703)943-1101 $–$$
In Waynesboro.

Rockfish Gap Outfitters (703)943-1461
Hours: 10 A.M. – 5 P.M.
This bicycle and outdoors shop is located 3 miles west on Highway 250 heading into town. If you need the services of a bike shop, take advantage of this one. The next accessible bike shop is 115 miles south on the Parkway in Roanoke.

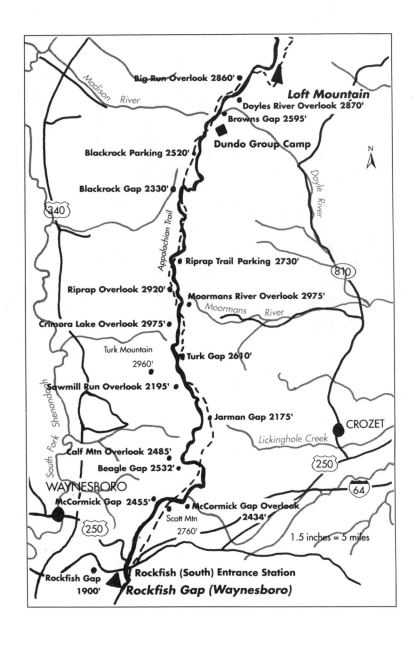

Big Run Overlook 2860'

Loft Mountain

Doyles River Overlook 2870'

Browns Gap 2595'

Dundo Group Camp

Blackrock Parking 2520'

N

Blackrock Gap 2330'

340

Appalachian Trail

Madison River

Doyle River

Riprap Trail Parking 2730'

Riprap Overlook 2920'

Moormans River Overlook 2975'

810

Moormans River

Crimora Lake Overlook 2975'

Turk Mountain 2960'

Turk Gap 2610'

Sawmill Run Overlook 2195'

Jarman Gap 2175'

CROZET

Lickinghole Creek

Calf Mtn Overlook 2485'

Beagle Gap 2532'

250

64

WAYNESBORO

South Fork Shenandoah

McCormick Gap 2455'

McCormick Gap Overlook 2434'

Scott Mtn 2760'

250

1.5 inches = 5 miles

Rockfish Gap 1900'

Rockfish (South) Entrance Station

Rockfish Gap (Waynesboro)

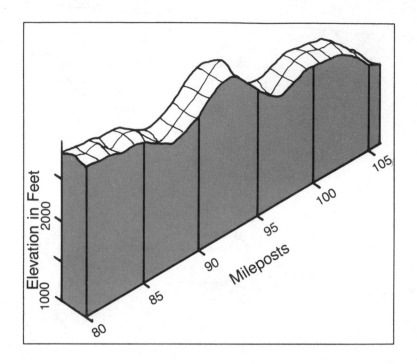

6 The
Blue Ridge
Parkway

With little fanfare, the Blue Ridge Parkway begins at Rockfish Gap and continues south for 470 miles. The mile markers still mark the terminus of the Parkway as 469 miles even though the construction of the Linn Cove Viaduct added an extra mile. Whereas the Skyline Drive is enclosed by national forests, the Parkway winds its way through some disparate geographic situations. The Parkway skirts around two fairly large cities, Roanoke and Asheville. Yet, the Parkway does take you through rugged wilderness areas, such as Shining Rock, Linville Gorge, and Pisgah National Forest. Any single day trip by bicycle along the Parkway can leave you with distinctly different impressions. One day you roll past cabbage patches and rust-colored barns; the next day your surroundings are craggy, rocky, and downright mountainous.

When you're speeding down the side of a mountain it's easy to experience sensory overload. Greens blur, the wind roars in your ears, and your adrenalin rises with a rush of feeling. The numerous, inevitable ascents of the Parkway, whether they be a quarter mile or 6 miles long, are the best times to take note of the flowers, animals, rocks, and trees that surround you.

Once again, trees dominate the natural scene in the Blue Ridge. David Catlin devotes an entire chapter to the integral role trees play in his book *A Naturalist's Blue Ridge Parkway*. He explains,

It is difficult to overstate the importance of trees in the natural history of the mountains, for trees greatly determine not only the kinds but the character of life here. It can even be legitimately claimed that trees put the 'Blue' in Blue Ridge, for hydrocarbons released into the atmosphere by the forest contribute to the characteristic haze on these mountains and to their distinctive color.

There are many distinct forests in the Blue Ridge. In the lower elevations there are oak-chestnut, cove hardwood, and oak-pine forests. The oak-chestnut forests are primarily white, northern red, black, scarlet, and chestnut oaks. The chestnut tree was once prominant along the Blue Ridge, but the chestnut blight fungus wiped out these valuable trees around the turn of the century.

Cove hardwood forests thrive in damp soils. These also feature tuliptrees, sugar maple, yellow buckeye, basswood, beech, yellow birch, northern red oak, and black cherry. Areas with good examples of cove hardwood forests include the James River Visitor Center and, closer to the Smokies, Standing Rock Overlook and Big Witch Tunnel.

Oak-pine forests exist in dryer, sandier soils, especially around the Asheville area. Species of southern Appalachian pines include white pine, shortleaf pine, pitch pine, Virginia pine, and Table Mountain pine.

In the higher elevations of 5,000 feet or more are northern hardwoods and spruce-fir forests. The northern hardwoods include trees found in the woods of Pennsylvania, New York, and New England. Beech, yellow buckeye, and yellow birch are all found.

The areas with spruce-fir forests are among the most memorable along the Parkway. Found in the very highest elevations, red spruce and Fraser fir are the distinctive inhabitants of Mt. Mitchell, Richland Balsam, and Waterrock Knob. Unfortunately environmental stresses, man-made and natural, are threatening these trees. The combined effects of the wooly aphid and acid rain have left total stands of dying

A Park Service sign puts Apple Orchard Mountain into better perspective. Photo by Elizabeth Skinner.

Fraser firs. The bone-white, leafless trunks and limbs are blatant reminders that environmental conditions are poor in the higher elevations.

The grass and heath balds along the Parkway are entirely devoid of trees. In areas like Craggy Gardens, there are entire mountainsides blanketed in rhododendron and mountain laurel. In May and June a day of cycling along the Parkway is a study in pinks, from pale to bold.

While we're on the subject of flowers, we would like to tell you when the most notable flowers bloom in the Blue Ridge, so you can be on the lookout.

Dogwood trees bloom from mid to late April.
Spring wildflowers bloom from late March to mid-May.
Flame azalea bloom a fantastic orange in May.

Mountain laurel bloom from late May through June.
Purple rhododendrum begin blooming in mid-June.
White rhododendrum bloom in June and July.

This schedule applies to the Skyline Drive as well. An excellent, detailed "Bloom Calendar" of wildflowers along the Parkway can be found in David Catlin's book *A Naturalist's Blue Ridge Parkway*. Mr. Catlin outlines peak bloom times and mileposts where specific flowers are most likely to be seen.

Much of the Parkway passes through wilderness areas, but scenes of rolling pasture and farmland also border the Parkway for mile upon mile. Roanoke Valley, much of Rocky Knob, Mabry Mill, Doughton Park, Boone and Blowing Rock consist of farmland. Cabbage and corn are the primary crops grown in these areas. Much of the open hillsides are used for grazing cattle.

Apple trees are common along the Parkway; there is one major orchard right alongside the Parkway between Linville Falls and Little Switzerland. Grapes are also grown in the Blue Ridge. The vineyards of Chateau Morrisette are visible along the mountainside between Rocky Knob and Mabry Mill.

With the Parkway's often narrow boundaries and its proximity to populated areas, you must be very attentive to spot wildlife while cycling along the Parkway. Whereas white-tailed deer are commonplace along the Skyline Drive, it is unusual to spot them along the Parkway. Deer are very skittish and bound off as soon as you approach them. That's one advantage of traveling by bicycle. You are quiet enough to get within close range of wildlife. Woodchuck and other small mammals often forage alongside the road. Once we set out on a dusk ride, intent upon spotting deer, and nearly wrecked trying to avoid a skunk that had wandered out onto the road. Time spent hiking or camping will reveal cottontail rabbits, raccoon, opposum and squirrels.

The bird that has fascinated us most along the Parkway is the hawk. Broad-winged and red-tailed hawks are the most common in the Blue Ridge. Often a quick break at an overlook becomes much more when hawks are sighted soaring on the thermal drafts that carry them for miles. With all this said about the flora and fauna along the the Parkway, there is one thing to remember. Elevation is the single overriding factor in bicycling the Parkway. It affects change in natural habitat, terrain, and weather. Elevation influences the road grades of the Parkway; elevation determines the type of forest you cycle past; elevation is a factor in the weather you encounter. There are journeys within journeys along the Parkway. One day you roll alongside pastures in the 1,000- to 2,000-foot range; another day yields the challenge of 5,000- to 6,000-foot mountains.

Rockfish Gap to Otter Creek

In the 115 miles from Rockfish Gap to Roanoke, the Blue Ridge narrows to a single ridgetop which the Parkway traverses, alternating from side to side. This 60-mile stretch begins with some stunning mountain overlooks. From Humpback Rocks Visitor Center the Parkway winds upward to the rocky vantage point of Raven's Roost. If you are traveling north, this is one of your first views of the Shenandoah Valley. The rock in this area, Catoctin greenstone, has a green tint and is part of the lava flows mentioned along the Skyline Drive. When we last stood on these rocks, the view was of the sun breaking through swift-moving clouds and mist slinking along the flint-gray ridges.

This section is memorable by bicycle for its wide, arcing switchbacks that are visible for miles ahead. The countryside varies from rocky cliffs to forests of hickory and chestnut oak and eastern hemlock to the pastures near the Whetstone Ridge wayside.

Highway 664 intersects the Parkway at Milepost 6. This road is very steep in both directions. There is one fine facility worth visiting, a private resort called Wintergreen. Although expensive, Wintergreen is open to the public and includes lodging, food, shops, horseback riding, swimming, tennis, and golf.

The road to Sherando Lake is up ahead at Milepost 16.5. Sherando is a beautiful state park, but you have to descend down the mountain to get there. It is 4.2 miles to the park entrance and 2 miles farther to the campground.

All told, the elevation varies quite a bit in this stretch. You reach the highest point north of the James River at 3,334 feet and descend to the James River which is the lowest elevation on the Parkway at 649 feet. This adds up to 4,802 feet climbed from Milepost 0 to Milepost 63. For those traveling north, the climb from the James River brings the total up to 5,990 feet.

If you are planning to make this stretch in one day, Whetstone Ridge may be a welcome breakpoint for travelers in either direction.

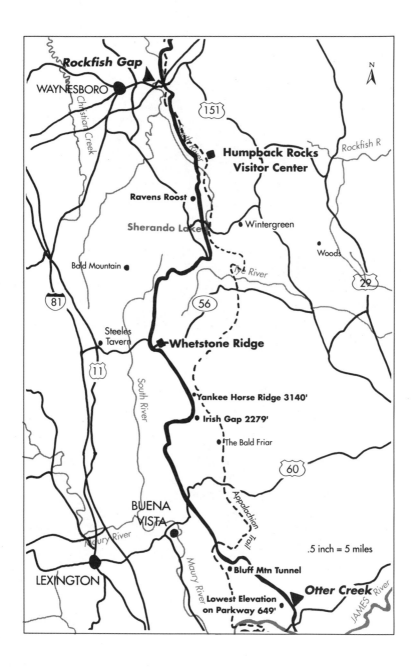

Rockfish Gap
WAYNESBORO
151
Humpback Rocks
Visitor Center
Rockfish R
Ravens Roost
Sherando Lake
Wintergreen
Woods
Bald Mountain
Tye River
29
81
56
Steeles
Tavern
Whetstone Ridge
11
South River
Yankee Horse Ridge 3140'
Irish Gap 2279'
The Bald Friar
60
BUENA
VISTA
Appalachian Trail
.5 inch = 5 miles
Maury River
LEXINGTON
Maury River
Bluff Mtn Tunnel
Otter Creek River
JAMES River
Lowest Elevation
on Parkway 649'

N

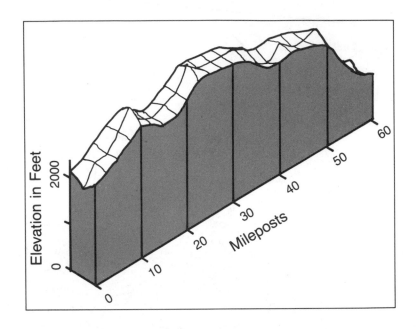

Milepost

6   **Humpback Rocks Visitor Center** (elev. 2,360 ft.)
             You may want to tour the working farm here. The
             facilities include water and restrooms. There is a
             ranger on duty.

10.7   **Raven's Roost** (elev. 3,200 feet)
             Take time to perch on these rocks and view the
             Shenandoah Valley.

13.5   **Wintergreen** $$$ (804)325-2200
             Wintergreen is open year-round. Proceed 1 mile east
             on Highway 664. Facilities include lodging, food, gift
             shops, and recreational facilities.

16.5   **Sherando Lake**
             This Virginia State Park is lovely, but it is a significant
             detour off the Parkway proper on Highway 814,
             involving a total of 6.2 miles one way. Entrance into

The view from Raven's Roost Overlook, elevation 3,200 feet. Photo by Elizabeth Skinner.

the park is $1.00 for bicyclists. The camping fee is $8.00 per campsite. You will find free hot showers at the bath house. A small camp store with limited hours sells basic food items.

Mountain Blue Crafts
If you are into handmade crafts and other mountain finds, this little log cabin is 1 mile off of the Parkway on Highway 814.

27   **Highway 56**
Although this highway involves steep descents in either direction, there are two campgrounds, one east, and one west, of the Parkway.

KOA Campground (703)377-2795
The KOA is located 1.5 miles on Highway 56 West.

*The Skyline Drive has many overlooks of the Shenanadoah Valley.
Photographer unknown.*

There is a gravel road upon entering the campground.
KOA has a store and laundry facilities.
Montebello Camping & Fishing (703)377-2066
This campground is located 2.5 miles on Highway 56
East. Facilities include a well-stocked camp store,
laundry, and showers.

29   **Whetstone Ridge Restaurant** (elev. 2,990 ft.)
This restaurant and gift shop makes a good lunch
stop.

54   **Bluff Mountain Tunnel** (elev. 7,630 ft.)
This is the first of many tunnels on the Parkway
heading south.

Sherando Lake invites you to take a cool swim after a hard day's ride.
Photo by Elizabeth Skinner.

60.8   **Otter Creek Campground & Restaurant** (elev.
777 ft.)
Otter Creek makes this one of the most pleasant
campgrounds on the Parkway. Facilities include a
restaurant, but no camp store. Take note that there is a
grocery store 4 miles farther south on Highway 501.
The campground has 42 tent sites and 26 trailer sites.

Otter Creek to Peaks of Otter

You will cross the James River just a few miles south of Otter Creek campground. The James River Visitor Center features a museum and a self-guided walking trail through the river locks system that was designed to accomodate horse-pulled barges through the Blue Ridge. The original plan, developed by George Washington, was to connect waterways that extended into Ohio. Ultimately railways replaced any earlier methods for transporting goods.

Since you are starting out at the lowest point on the Parkway and heading toward the highest point on the Parkway in Virginia expect to do some climbing. Uphill climbs will amount to right at 4,000 feet. That's quite a bit for a mere twenty-five miles.

Midway into your ascent you will encounter Thunder Ridge at 3,845 feet. This is a thickly forested area of northern red oak and Carolina hemlock. From here you will cycle past stands of striped and mountain maple at the overlook of Arnold's Valley. The Appalachian Trail parallels the Parkway throughout this section and crosses it once at Milepost 74.9.

Certainly one reason for the popularity of Peaks of Otter is its proximity to numerous hiking trails. Peaks of Otter is one of the most extensive facilities on the Parkway. The lodge and restaurant have a simple mountain elegance from the gray-stained exterior to the high ceilings and exposed beams of the dining room. Views of Sharp Top and Flat Top mountains provide the crowning touch. Peaks of Otter was named after the headwaters of the Otter River which originate from the twin peaks. Peaks of Otter has a large campground with a modest camp store. The camp store serves sandwiches and stocks basic canned goods, ice cream, and beverages. Expect a fair amount of traffic in this area.

Milepost

63.6　　**James River Visitor Center** (elev. 668 ft.)

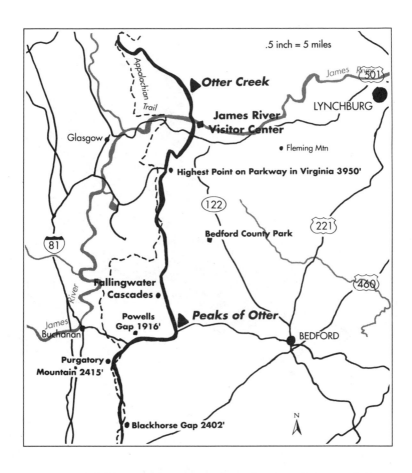

Make sure you take time out for the exhibits and the self-guided nature trail to the river locks.

63.7   **H & H Food Market & Restaurant**
Take U.S. 501 1 mile toward Big Island. This is a well-stocked grocery store. If you are heading north, this is a good place to stock up.

85.7   **Peaks of Otter Lodge** (703)586-1081 $$ – $$$ (elev. 2,525 ft.)

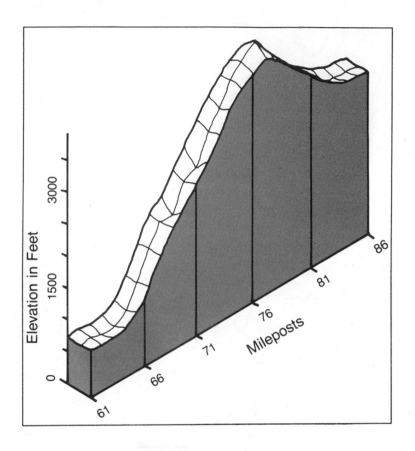

Peaks of Otter Lodge is the only lodge on the Parkway open year round. Facilities here include a restaurant, coffee shop, gift shop, and visitor center.

86   **Highway 43 South**
Exit left toward Bedford, Virginia.
Peaks of Otter Campground (elev. 2,875 ft.)
The campground is equipped with a camp store for grocery items, beverages, and sandwiches. The campground has 90 tent sites and 53 trailer sites.
Otter's Den Bed & Breakfast (703) 586-2204 $$$
Proceed 2.2 miles on Hwy. 43 South.

Taking stock at Peaks of Otter Wayside. Photo by Elizabeth Skinner.

Peaks of Otter to Roanoke Mountain

It is 35 miles from Peaks of Otter to Roanoke Mountain. The city of Roanoke sits in a valley, so the majority of this section is downhill. With both an airport and bus service, Roanoke is a possible beginning or ending point for a tour of the Blue Ridge. If you are on an extended tour, Roanoke is the place to seek assistance for any major difficulties. Roanoke's population is over 220,000, which makes it the largest city directly off of the Parkway.

There are numerous access roads from the Parkway into the Roanoke area. We have investigated each side road in order to recommend the best ways to safely travel by bike into the city. If you plan to camp at Roanoke Mountain campground, you may want to get off of the Parkway either north or south of the campground in order to stock up on food. For those seeking motels, there are several possibilities. We discovered an excellent bicycle route into downtown Roanoke (described below). Downtown Roanoke boasts a farmer's market, museums, shops and restaurants.

The best selection of motels directly off of the parkway is 1.5 miles down Highway 220 North. Be careful, though, Highway 220 is a major highway with heavy truck traffic. Fortunately, you can pick up a frontage road just a mile north which is a direct route to most facilities.

The most accessible bicycle shop in the Roanoke area is best accessed from the Vinton, Virginia Parkway exit on Highway 24.

For anyone considering flying in or out of Roanoke, you should be forewarned that the airport is on the extreme north end of the city. We do not have a route to recommend from the airport to the Parkway. The most direct route is Highway 220. If you know you will be cycling from the airport to the Parkway, we suggest you write for a city map from the Roanoke Valley Convention and Visitors Bureau.

The Parkway assumes a different character in the Roanoke area. In the Roanoke Valley, mountains are replaced by rolling farmland and the presence of a major city. Residential areas are visible from the

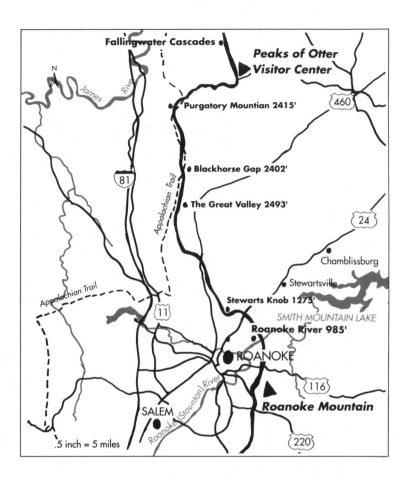

Parkway. A true-blue naturalist might scoff at the Roanoke area, yet the opportunity to bicycle in the Blue Ridge at all is a compromise between people, their technology, and nature.

For an appreciation of the city, we recommend taking in the view from the overlook at Mill Mountain Park, just a mile from Roanoke Mountain Campground. There is a pleasant nature trail at Milepost 115, called Roanoke River Overlook, where native trees are identified. They include chestnut oak, eastern hemlock, black locust,

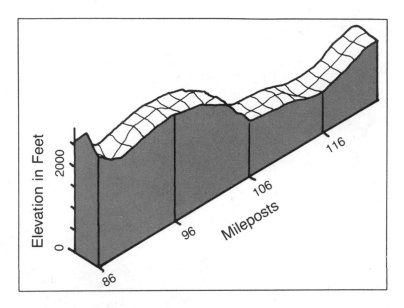

sassafras, scarlet oak, and white pine. The trail culminates in an overlook of the Roanoke River.

For anyone traveling north to Peaks of Otter, the going is uphill. Since you are climbing up out of the Roanoke Valley, you will gain a total of 2,608 feet. Make sure you save some energy for the last five miles into Peaks of Otter, a tough stretch of steep road.

Milepost

112.2   **Vinton, Virginia**

Vinton is a good place to stock up to camp at Roanoke Mountain. Take Highway 24 West eight-tenths of a mile toward Roanoke to the East Vinton Plaza. Highway 24 is a four-lane divided highway with a small shoulder. The East Vinton Plaza has everything; you can find a medical clinic a half mile farther on Highway 24.

Cardinal Bicycle (703) 345-1687
From the Vinton exit follow Highway 24 West for 1.8
miles. Continue straight on Washington Ave.
(Highway 24 turns left). (It becomes Gus Nicks Blvd.)
At 3.6 miles turn right onto Orange Ave. and proceed
.5 miles to Cardinal Bicycle on the right.

115 **Roanoke River Overlook** (elev. 985)
It's a 20 minute walk on the Roanoke River Trail to an
overlook of the river.

120.5 **Mill Mountain Road**
Mill Mountain Road takes you to Roanoke Mountain
campground, Mill Mountain Park, Roanoke Memorial
Hospital, and downtown Roanoke. Because cycling in
a large city is safest when you're in the know, we were
determined to find the best route into Roanoke.
Ultimately, the road becomes a marked bicycle route
as it parallels the Roanoke River. There is one thing
we want to caution you about. This route is all
downhill going into the city and all uphill going back
to the Parkway. Now is the time to have an enlight-
ened attitude about climbing hills.
What follows are our best directions into Roanoke.
Turn onto Mill Mountain Road at Milepost 120.4 on
the Parkway. Follow Mill Mountain Road up, around,
and down the mountain. First you will pass Roanoke
Mountain Campground on the left at 1.2 miles; Mill
Mountain Park is 1.2 miles beyond the campground at
2.4 miles. Then you will descend down the mountain
into Roanoke. Mill Mountain Road becomes Walnut
Street. At 4.4 miles turn left onto Belleview Avenue.
You will see a Gate gas station on the corner.
Belleview cuts through the middle of the Roanoke
Memorial Hospital complex at 5 miles, and soon you
will see bike route signs. Belleview bears right onto
Wiley Drive. Wiley Drive follows alongside the

Roanoke River and passes through Smith Park and over the Roanoke River twice. At the second bridge take the next left over the railroad crossing onto Winoa Street. The next street is Main Street. Turn right on Main Street to head downtown.

Roanoke Mountain Campground

Roanoke Mountain Campground is 1.2 miles off of the Parkway on Mill Mountain Road. The only facilities here are bathrooms. There is a ranger on duty. The campground has 74 tent sites and 31 trailer sites.

Mill Mountain Park (elev. 1747)

Mill Mountain Park is located 2.4 miles from the Parkway. It features a zoological park, a wildflower garden, and an overlook with an outstanding view of Roanoke and the Roanoke Valley. The park has a snack bar and restrooms, and is open April through November.

Roanoke Memorial Hospital

This hospital is located 5 miles from the Parkway along our suggested route into the city.

Holiday Inn South (703)343-0121 $$$

This Holiday Inn is conveniently seen from about 6 miles into the route to Roanoke on Wiley Drive. The street address is 1927 Franklin Road.

121.4 **Highway 220 North**

Highway 220 North is a major highway with heavy truck traffic. Remember, proceed with caution. It is 1.4 miles to a frontage road which will take you to numerous motels and restaurants.

Colony House Motor Lodge (703)345-0411 $$

Econo Lodge (703)774-1621 $

Holiday Inn (703)343-0121 $$$

121.2 **Highway 220 South**

If all you need is a motel, there are two motels within a mile of the Parkway on Highway 220 South.

Parkway Motel and Restaurant (703) 989-6194 $
Apple Valley Motel (703) 989-0675 $

Roanoke Mountain to Rocky Knob

One of the best things about the climb south, out of Roanoke, is that you have plenty of time to appreciate the views of Roanoke Valley. Between Mileposts 128 and 133 the Parkway climbs 1,800 feet with a 6.8 percent grade. Your breakfast will be long gone by the time you reach Smart View at Milepost 154.5. You can tell little about road grades along this stretch from studying the Parkway map. It is not safe to assume that, since Rocky Knob is at 3,572 feet and Roanoke is at 1,425 feet, you will have smooth sailing traveling north into Roanoke. Although the map leads you to expect a drop in elevation of 2,147 feet, the Parkway actually rises and descends numerous times.

There are some tough, but brief, climbs traveling north from Rocky Knob to Roanoke. Likewise, these climbs make for welcome descents for those heading south. Overall, there are two major climbs from Roanoke to Rocky Knob. The first major climb begins about six miles out of Roanoke. The second major climb begins around Rakes Millpond at Milepost 162.4 and ends beyond the Rocky Knob Campground at about Milepost 169.

There are two places on this stretch convenient for food and shelter: Highway 221 at Adney Gap and Highway 8 at Tuggle Gap. These would be good places to stock up on supplies or have breakfast or lunch.

One warning about road conditions for this section: watch out for potholes and patched sections. This is especially critical along the descents on this stretch. The quality of road surface for this section is below the norm for the Parkway.

Although the pavement is rough, we want to stress how lovely the Rocky Knob area is. Its grassy knobs are similar to those of Scotland. The huge, protruding boulders and rocks are a farmer's nightmare. The pastoral setting of Rocky Knob would be a great place to set up an easel and canvas, or to simply stand and feel the energy of the wind.

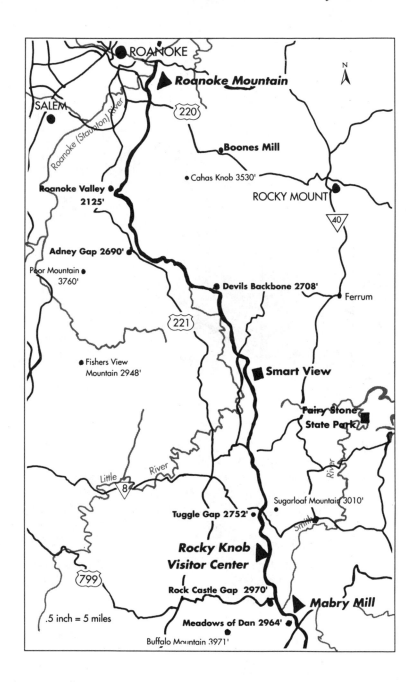

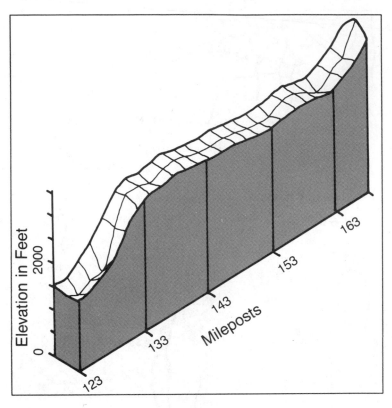

Milepost

136   **Adney Gap** (elev. 2,690 ft.)

Take the spur road four-tenths of a mile to Highway 221. You will find facilities on the left and the right. This is an easy exit. There are no descents or climbs of note.

Powell's Convenience Store

This country store, on your immediate left, has a good supply of groceries.

Hours: Monday-Sunday 6:30 A.M.–10:30 P.M.

The Pantry Restaurant

Turn right off the spur road onto Highway 221 and

Take a load off and chew the fat with the locals at Bus Shoppe Snacks. Photo by Elizabeth Skinner.

cycle four-tenths of a mile for breakfast or lunch. This restaurant has limited hours: Monday–Sunday 8 A.M.– 4 P.M. (closed Thursday).

147.5   **Bus Shoppe Snacks**

Is it open? Take a load off, and chew the fat with the locals. This converted school bus has beverages, snacks, and basic grocery items. Bus Shoppe Snacks is visible from the Parkway on State Route 678.

154.5   **Smart View**

Smart View is a lovely picnic area with lots of shade for a hot summer day. Restrooms and water are available here.

159.5   **Craft Store**
We only know this place as the Craft Store. It is visible from the Parkway. You will find quilts, pillows and knick-knacks for sale.

165.3   **Tuggle Gap** (elev. 2,752 ft.)
Exit onto Highway 8 and turn left. Proceed 150 yards.
Tuggle Gap Restaurant & Motel (703)745-3402 $
This place doesn't look like much, but they serve good food. The motel is very small.

167   **Rocky Knob Campground** (elev. 3,572)
Rocky Knob is among our favorite Parkway camp-grounds. You will find an excellent trail system here. A short, but steep walk to the top of Rocky Knob affords an excellent view. (Watch out for cow patties.) The campground has 81 tent sites and 28 trailer sites.

Rocky Knob to Mabry Mill

There are a mere 9 miles between Rocky Knob and Mabry Mill, but the Parkway moves through the high knobs of the Rocky Knob area, then swings down to Mabry Mill in one memorable swoop. If you are traveling south and camping at Rocky Knob, we suggest you rouse yourself early, break camp, and cycle the vigorous 9 miles to Mabry Mill for buckwheat pancakes. Arrive at Mabry Mill by 8 a.m. to avoid standing in line.

If you are traveling north, the climbs into Rocky Knob are rewarding. The most memorable climb of this section reveals itself as a wide, rising arc in full view of the climber.

The big surprise of this section is Chateau Morrisette. Who would be expecting a winery in these parts? Chateau Morrisette is less than a mile off of the Parkway at Milepost 171. This is the only winery that we know of in such close proximity to the Parkway. Take some time out for a tour of the winery and, by all means, the wine tasting.

Mabry Mill is a certified "scenic" spot on the Parkway. Reported to be the most photographed sight on the Parkway, it is nearly always crowded with people. Beware of traffic when approaching the area. Mabry Mill is popular for good reason—a tour of the mill is fascinating. They still grind cornmeal and buckwheat flour, which can be purchased. Also on exhibit are a moonshine still, a sorghum mill, and a soap-making kettle. On a summer day, you may even chance upon a musician or two playing the hammered dulcimer, banjo or mandolin.

Milepost

171   **Chateau Morrisette Winery** (703)593-2865

Just past Milepost 171 look for State Route 726 where you will turn right if traveling south. Make an immediate left onto State Route 777 (Winery Road). The winery is less than a quarter-mile from here. The

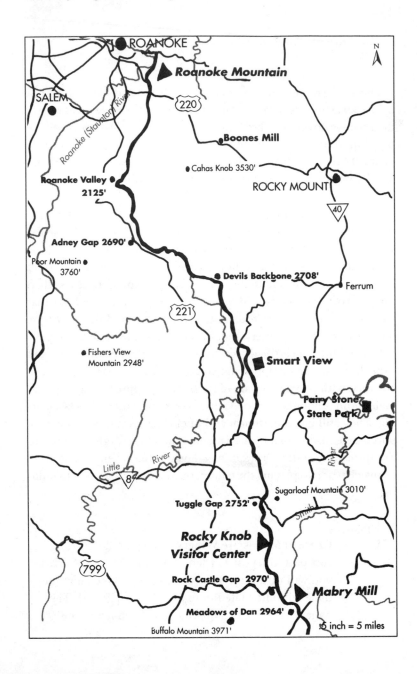

ROANOKE

Roanoke Mountain

SALEM

220

Roanoke (Stanton) River

Boones Mill

Cahas Knob 3530'

Roanoke Valley
2125'

ROCKY MOUNT

40

Adney Gap 2690'

Poor Mountain
3760'

Devils Backbone 2708'

Ferrum

221

Fishers View
Mountain 2948'

■ **Smart View**

Fairy Stone
State Park

River

Little

8

River

Sugarloaf Mountain 3010'

Smith

Tuggle Gap 2752'

Rocky Knob
Visitor Center

799

Rock Castle Gap 2970'

Mabry Mill

Meadows of Dan 2964'

Buffalo Mountain 3971'

1/2 inch = 5 miles

N

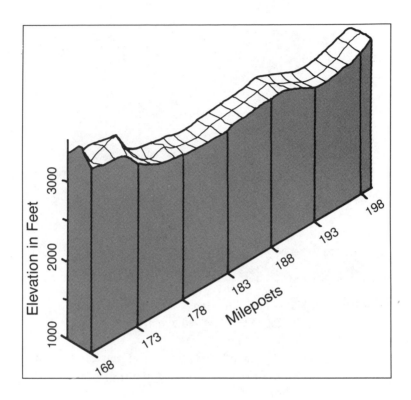

winery is open for tours Monday-Friday 10 A.M.– 5
P.M.; Saturday 10 A.M.– 5 P.M.; Sunday 12 noon– 5 P.M.
Lunch and dinner are served.

174   **Rocky Knob Cabins**   (703)593-3503 $$
These cabins are just off the Parkway at Milepost 174,
reservations are necessary. They are equipped with
electric kitchens, running water, linens, dishes, and
utensils.

Woodberry Inn   (703)593-2567 $$$
Traveling south on the Parkway, turn left onto State
Route 758E at the Rocky Knob Cabins exit. Self-
described as a "hideaway resembling an old inn in

The gristmill at Mabry Mill still grinds the grain for buckwheat flour, corn meal, and grits. Photo by Elizabeth Skinner.

northern Scotland," this place has all the touches. The Inn also features a homestyle buffet restaurant.

176.2   Mabry Mill (elev. 2,855 ft.)

Mabry Mill is open May 1 through October 31. In addition to the mill and exhibits, you will find a gift shop and restaurant here. Bathrooms, drinking water, and a telephone are available.

Restaurant hours: 8:30 A.M. – 7:30 P.M. daily.

The Appalachians abound with folk artists such as this hammered dulcimer player at Mabry Mill. Photo by Elizabeth Skinner.

Mabry Mill to Fancy Gap

The town of Meadows of Dan is just 1 mile south of Mabry Mill. Here you will find ample facilities: groceries, a laundry, restaurants, and lodging.

Relative to other sections, this 23-mile stretch is not very demanding. There is one notable climb approaching Groundhog Mountain a little over a mile long. Groundhog Mountain has an elevation of 3,030 feet. You might want to take a break here, climb to the top of the observation tower, and study the various types of fences on display: snake rail, buck rail, and post and rail.

From Groundhog Mountain, the road rolls out toward Fancy Gap with no big surprises. The Parkway drops slightly, and you will find a straightaway of considerable length through the Orchard Gap area. Orchard Gap Deli is visible to the left.

We have two great sensory impressions of this area. One is the pungent aroma from the many fields of cabbage ready for harvest in September; the other is an abundance of flame azalea which blooms bright orange in May.

There is a slight climb into Fancy Gap where the elevation is 2,925 feet. Fancy Gap, visible to either side of the Parkway, is an obvious stopping place for those camping or needing a motel. For some, the distance between the Park Service campgrounds of Rocky Knob and Doughton Park will be further than you want to push in one day. It all depends on pace, and where you are in your trip. Before you pass up the facilities at Fancy Gap, keep in mind that there are roughly 9 miles of steady climbing into Doughton Park.

Milepost

177.7   **Meadows of Dan, Virginia** (elev. 2,960 ft.)
Meadows of Dan is visible to either side of the Parkway. You will find restaurants, a grocery store, and a laundry.

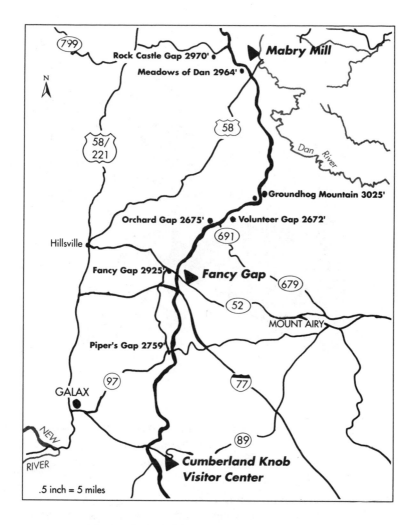

Blue Ridge Motel (703)952-2244 $
This motel is located 75 yards west on U.S. Highway
58.

180 Spangler's Bed and Breakfast (703)952-2454 $-$$
Harold and Trudy Spangler have stories of many

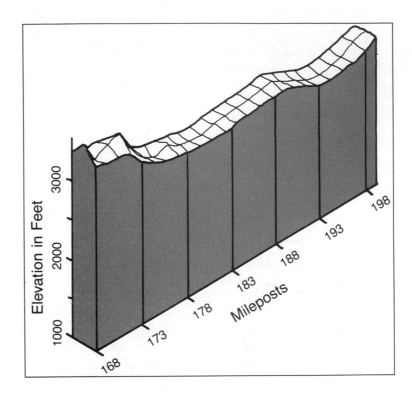

bicyclists who stayed there. To find their lovely house, be on the lookout for State Route 600 to your left heading south. It is just down the road from the Mayberry Trading Post on State Route 602. If you get confused, ask there.

180.5   **Mayberry Trading Post**
On your left traveling south, this general store is well-stocked with groceries and baked goods. On occasion, we have enjoyed mountain music here.

188.8   **Groundhog Mountain** (elev. 3,025 ft.)
Groundhog Mountain has an observation tower, and features a display of the various types of fences

The Parkway makes a quick ascent to Groundhog Mountain. Photo by Elizabeth Skinner.

189   **Doe Run Lodge and Restaurant** (703) 398-2212 $$$
Visible from the Parkway, Doe Run features suites and
villas with daily and weekly rates. Facilities include
tennis courts, pool and restaurant.
constructed along the Parkway. You will find a picnic
area, bathrooms, and drinking water.

193.7   **Orchard Gap Deli** (elev. 2,675 ft.)
This Deli has sandwiches and a good selection of
groceries. Open year round.
Hours: Monday–Saturday 7 A.M.–7 P.M.; Sunday
8 A.M.– 6 P.M.

199.4   **Fancy Gap, Virginia** (elev. 2,925 ft.)
Fancy Gap is visible to either side of the Parkway.

Motels, restaurants, a campground, and post office are all here.

Fox Trail Campground (703)728-7776
Go 500 yards west on Highway 683. You will see signs for camping. This excellent campground is open year round. Facilities include: showers, laundry, camp store, ice, and telephone.

Mountain Top Restaurant & Motel (703)728-9414 $
Open year-round.

Lake View Motel & Restaurant (703)728-7841 $
Open year-round.

Fancy Gap to Cumberland Knob

You will cross from Virginia into North Carolina along this section. As you pedal along a shady, winding stretch of road, the Parkway makes a seamless transition from one state to the other. Upon leaving Fancy Gap you will encounter a fairly steep climb of about a mile. It is an equal proposition of up and down all the way to Cumberland Knob.

We made up the term "rolling mountain" while cycling this section. When you look at the road, you just know you'll be cycling rolling hills, the kind that leave you enough momentum to crest the hill ahead of you, but this is rarely the case. Instead, you end up shifting down in the face of a climb, whether it be short or long.

This section of the Parkway is mostly pasture and farmland spread out across rolling hills. Cattle graze on small knobs with farmhouses frequently within view. Small streams trickle haphazardly alongside the Parkway. There's a timeless, down-home feel to this landscape.

Cumberland Knob was the first park constructed on the Parkway. It makes a good break point, or starting point if you are day-tripping.

One big surprise in this section is the presence of an American Youth Hostel. There is no other hostel along the Skyline Drive or the Parkway. Unless you are a member of AYH you probably would not know this is here. It is secluded on a wonderful piece of property just off of the Parkway. The house is charming, with all the comforts of home and a great deck in the back.

Milepost

206.5   **Felts Brothers Grocery**
Just a half mile off of the Parkway, heading south on the Parkway turn right onto State Route 608, then left on State Route 620 to Highway 97 North. Hours: Monday–Friday 6 A.M. – 8 P.M.; Saturday 8 A.M. – 6 P.M.; closed Sunday.

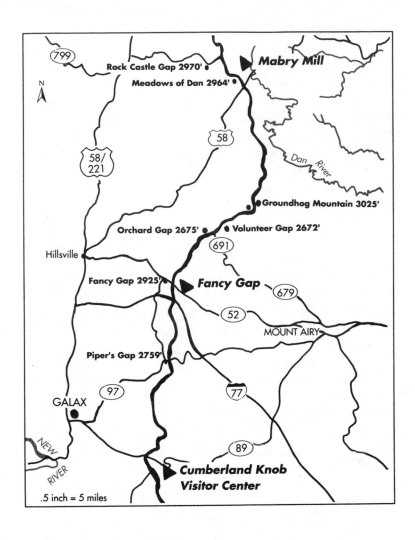

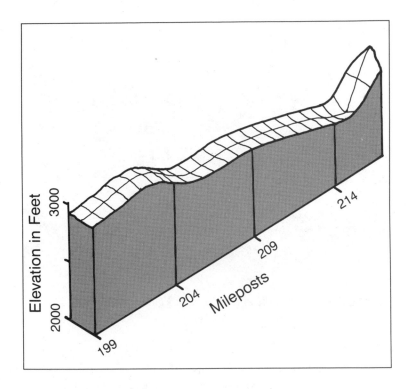

214.5   **Blue Ridge Country American Youth Hostel**
(703)236-4962
This is truly a lovely place, and you don't have to be a
member to stay here. You do need to bring your own
food. The entrance is not marked. Look for a paved
road to your left heading south.

215.8   **Virginia Route 89**
D & R Grocery
Proceed 1 mile North on Route 89.
International Deli and Bakery
Proceed .4 miles South on Route 89. Limited hours.

Blue Ridge Country is the only American Youth Hostel on the Parkway. Photo by Elizabeth Skinner.

217.5   **Cumberland Knob** (elev. 2,885 ft.)
There is no camping or food here. You will find restrooms, drinking water, and a picnic area. There is a small gift shop where a ranger is on duty. A brief trail system features a hike along Gully Creek with views of the Piedmont.

Cumberland Knob to Doughton Park

From Cumberland Knob you will encounter rolling hills with panoramic views of the Piedmont to the east. Pastureland, meadows, and apple orchards comprise much of the next thirteen miles. Milepost 221.5 to Milepost 230.1 is relatively flat. This is one of the rare straightaways on the Parkway where cycling is a breeze—enjoy. Big Pine Creek meanders from one side of the Parkway to the other. Little Glade Pond (Milepost 230.1) marks a change in terrain. This is a pleasant break point before heading out for the climb into Doughton Park. Conversely, it makes a great place to regroup after tearing down out of the mountains from Doughton Park.

From Little Glade Pond (elev. 2,709 ft.), the Parkway begins a steady 1,000-foot climb which crests at Air Bellows Gap (elev. 3,729 ft.). The terrain undergoes a subtle metamorphosis from farmland to mountain as you approach the Doughton Park area. Instead of grassy meadows you begin to cycle past sheer rock face. Doughton Park is one of the larger parks in land area. Although you're only in the 3,000- to 4,000-foot range, south of the lodge the road will thrill you as it cuts right through mountain, and you shoot past a high rock wall where the mountain was blasted to make way for the road.

Beware of gaps throughout this entire area where gusting winds may be encountered. Cycling through gaps at high speeds can be tricky.

Signs announce Doughton Park well before facilities are encountered. Heading south, Brinegar Cabin (Milepost 238.5) is the first point of interest. The campground is next at Milepost 239.3. Deer sightings are a daily occurrence at Doughton Park, especially at dawn and dusk. The meadow north of the campground is a likely spot.

If you stay overnight at Doughton Park, a climb to Bluff Mountain overlook on the trail system should give you a fine appreciation of the feat you are accomplishing by cycling the Parkway. South from the rocky ledge of Bluff Mountain the highway winds uphill through

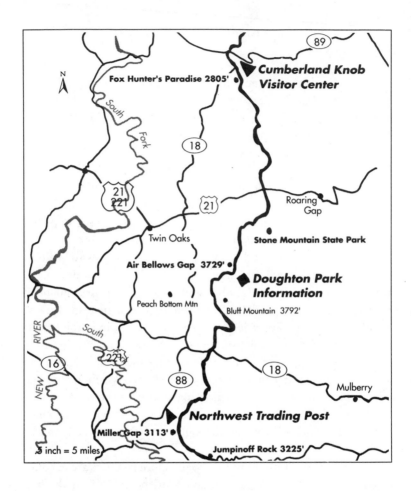

decidedly mountainous terrain. In fact, cycling from either direction into Doughton Park is a challenge.

Milepost

218.6   **Fox Hunters Paradise** (elev. 2,805 ft.)
This overlook has excellent views of the Piedmont.

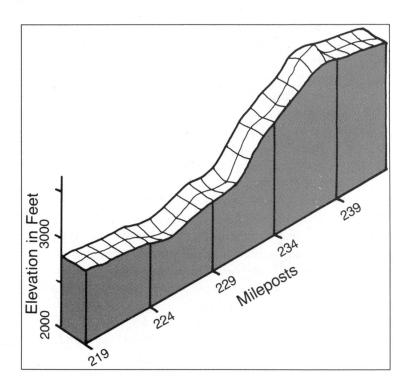

229   **Highway 21** intersects here.
Brush Creek Country Store
Just 1.3 miles south of the Parkway toward Roaring
Gap, this store is well worth the side trip if you need
supplies. There is no major climb or descent. Open
year round.
Hours: Monday–Saturday 7 A.M.–9 P.M.; Sunday 10
a.m.–9 P.M.
Roaring Gap Motel & Restaurant (919)363-2666 $
This modest motel is 2.7 miles south on Highway 21.
Restaurant hours: Monday–Saturday 7 A.M. – 9 P.M.;
closed Sunday.

Marion's Old Homeplace
Marion's is 3 miles north on Highway 21. They have
excellent home-style food. Turn right on Glade Valley
Road. The restaurant is well-marked by signs. There
are no major hills or descents but the road is well
traveled.
Open May 1–October 31.
Hours: Wednesday–Friday 5 P.M. – 8:30 P.M.
Saturday 4 P.M. – 8:30 P.M.; Sunday 12 noon –
8:30 P.M.

Sparta, North Carolina
Sparta is 7 miles north on Highway 21. This well-
traveled road has truck traffic. There are a few big hills
coming into Sparta. If you want a diversion or you
need special services, this may be a good time to divert
off the Parkway. Sparta has banks, laundry facilities, a
hospital, and a hardware store.

Alleghany Inn (919)372-2501 $
Through town on Highway 21; open year round.

231.5   **Mountain Hearth Bed and Breakfast** $$
(919)372-8743
This charming bed and breakfast is 200 yards off the
Parkway. Turn left at State Route 1109. With breakfast
included, the rates are very reasonable. The proprie-
tors also run a restaurant, a bakery, and an antique
store. The restaurant serves breakfast, lunch, and
dinner as they coincide with the stated hours.
Hours: Tuesday–Saturday 12 noon–8 P.M.; Sunday 9
A.M.–2 P.M. Closed Monday.

238.6 –
244.8   **Doughton Park**
Doughton Park announces itself way before any
facilities are encountered. There is an excellent 12-
mile trail system here.

Approaching Air Bellows Gap, a good spot for studying wildflowers in the summer and bright red mountain ash in the fall. Photo by Charlie Skinner.

239.2   **Doughton Park Campground**
This Park Service campground is separated from the restaurant and lodge by two steep miles. There is a hiking trail connecting the two facilities. There are 110 tent sites and 25 trailer sites in the campground.

241.1   **Bluffs Lodge and Coffee Shop**   (919)372-4499 $$$
Restaurant hours: Monday–Sunday 7:30 A.M.–7:30 P.M.

Doughton Park to Northwest Trading Post

From the lodge and restaurant at Doughton Park, there are several miles of spectacular mountain scenery and cycling territory. One of the big thrills for us is the visibility you have of the path the Parkway takes before you actually cycle it. Where the Parkway cuts alongside Bluff Mountain, water trickles down gray-black rock that extends fifty feet up from the side of the road. It's fun to imagine what that same rock looks like in January after a few long, hard freezes. Through the winter months the entire side of the mountain is covered in glimmering ice, inches thick.

Once out of the park, the road makes a rapid descent toward Laurel Springs. There are several miles of level cycling on the way to Laurel Springs. Laurel Springs is a touristy dot on the map with a few good facilities, and some not so good. Miller's Campground is located roughly 1 mile before Laurel Springs.

Once past Laurel Springs, the Parkway climbs again. The terrain is basically rolling mountain with a few hills you can actually crest without shifting down.

If you enjoy checking out the local culture, Glendale Springs is the real treat of this area. The Church of the Frescoes and Glendale Springs Inn & Restaurant lend quaint charm to this community. Inside the Church of the Frescoes are life-sized paintings of "The Lord's Supper" and other religious scenes. A sunny country garden filled with such flowers as zinnias, day lilies, poppies, and daisies surrounds the church. There is also an elaborate herb garden centered around two harps in town. One of these is an aeolian harp designed to be played by the wind.

The Northwest Trading Post is a co-op for North Carolina craftsmen. You must stop here, even if you do not venture into Glendale Springs. The Trading Post is crammed with quilts and other handcrafted items, such as lamp shades decorated with pressed wildflowers, knitted afghans and sweaters, and wind chimes. The

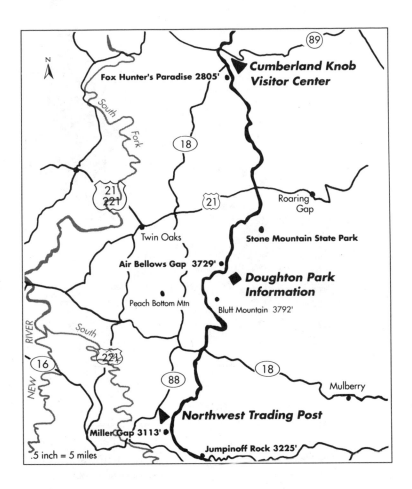

various home-made baked goods are delicious. There are country ham biscuits, hummingbird cake, molasses stack cake, peanut butter and oatmeal cookies, German chocolate cake, hoop cheese, dried apples, and more.

With camping, lodging, and so much to see, you might want to plan to make an early day of it here.

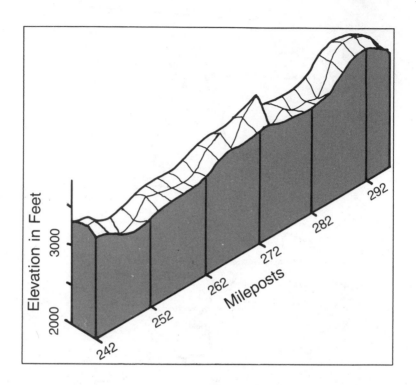

Milepost

247   **Miller's Camping** (919)359-8156
           Visible to the right traveling south, Miller's Camping
           is open April 1 through November. Facilities include
           showers, laundry, ice, and a camp store.

248   **Laurel Springs, North Carolina**
           Laurel Springs is visible to the right of the Parkway
           traveling south.
           Tree Top Motor Lodge (919)359-2231 $
           Open year round, this motel also runs a well-stocked
           grocery store.
           Buck & Doe Lodge (919)359-2221 $

Post and rail fences line the Parkway at the southern end of Doughton Park. Photo by Charlie Skinner.

256   **Mountain View Lodge and Cabins** (919) 982-2233 $$
Options include one and two bedroom cabins with
kitchenettes. Breakfast is served in the lodge.

259   **Northwest Trading Post** (919)982-2543
Open May 1 through October 31, the Trading Post has
home-made crafts and baked goods made by North
Carolina craftsmen.

259   **Glendale Springs, North Carolina**
There is very little indication from the Parkway of the
bounty that is Glendale Springs. This is a perfect
example of what can lie just yards beyond the Park-

way. Turn right and head south at the Northwest
Trading Post.

Lee's Lodge & Restaurant (919)982-3289 $
Glendale Springs Inn & Bakery (919)982-2103 $$$
Raccoon Holler Campground (919)982-2706
Raccoon Holler is 1 mile into Glendale Springs, just
follow the signs. Facilities include showers, laundry,
and a camp store with grocery items.

Church of the Frescoes
In the center of town; Fresco art includes "The Lord's
Supper," "Mary Great With Child," and "St. John the
Baptist."

The Church of the Frescoes' unassuming exterior belies the mystery within. Photo by Elizabeth Skinner.

Tired of camping? Pamper yourself at Glendale Springs Inn and Restaurant. Photo by Charlie Skinner.

Northwest Trading Post to Julian Price Memorial Park

There is no level ground here. You climb from the Northwest Trading Post, descend some, and then climb some more. You are headed toward Boone, Blowing Rock, and Grandfather Mountain, so higher elevations, and the climbs that accompany them, are inevitable.

There are several fine overlooks in this area, so at least cruise through them: View From the Lump (Milepost 64.4), Mt. Jefferson Overlook (Milepost 266.9), and Elk Mountain Overlook (Milepost 274.3). At E. B. Jeffress Park there is a brief trail to Cascades waterfall.

In the 37 miles between the Northwest Trading Post and Julian Price, the Parkway takes you through a busy area. Those traveling south are approaching a spectacular section of the Parkway. Boone and Blowing Rock are major tourist areas. Blowing Rock is far more accessible to the Parkway than Boone. It has numerous motels with a wide price range and several excellent restaurants. Boone does offer one service that Blowing Rock does not—it has a bike shop. Boone is a great town, but it is not necessary to travel that far since Blowing Rock is so close.

There is a fun way into Boone, via Flannery Fork Road, if you are traveling on a mountain bike or have tires tough enough to withstand several miles of gravel road. See our directions that follow.

To be sure, this is a great area for mountain bikes. At Moses H. Cone Memorial Park there are over 20 miles of carriage paths that wander around the estate. Moses H. Cone is a grand estate with a stately manor house perched on a hilltop that looks down upon a man-made lake. The house and estate were donated to the Park Service. The carriage trails are used for hiking, horseback riding, and cross-country skiing. Although these trails would be ideal for mountain biking, the official policy is a firm ban on bikes. The manor house

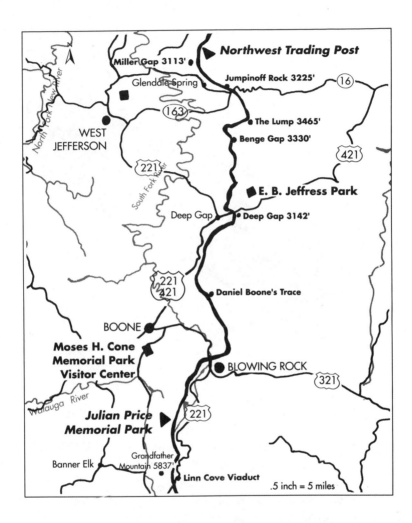

is used as a gift shop for mountain crafts and pottery. The handicrafts at Moses H. Cone are very fine and come with expensive price tags. A vast array of pottery and hand-blown glassware, scarves and shawls made of fine wools, quilted clothing, and funky jewelry make you wish for more room in your bike bags.

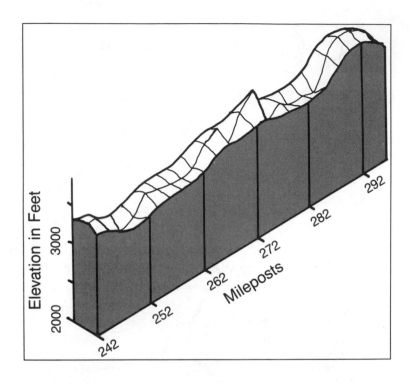

At Julian Price Memorial Park you will want to be sure to get a campsite along Price Lake. If you have the time you might want to fish for some rainbow trout or rent a canoe to go exploring. A hike around the lake after a full day of cycling would be a good way to work the kinks out.

If you do camp at Julian Price, you can find food just a mile south of the campground on the access road to Highway 221.

Milepost

268   **Benge Gap**   (elev. 3,296 ft.)
             If you're headed south you could shoot past Benge
             Gap and miss the motel, store, and restaurant here. Be
             on the lookout to your right.

Park Vista Motel, Country Store & Restaurant
(919)877-2750 $–$$

271.9   E. B. Jeffress Park (elev. 3,570 ft.)
This park is primarily a picnic area with drinking
water and restrooms. Cascades Nature Trail is a 30-
minute hike to the falls.

276.4   Deep Gap (elev. 3,142 ft.)
U.S. Highway 421 intersects the Parkway here. It is
one mile toward Boone to several convenience stores.
U.S. Highway 421 is a heavily traveled two-lane road.
We do not advise going into Boone this way.

291.9   U.S. Highway 221 and U.S. Highway 321
Boone and Blowing Rock can be accessed by exiting
here.

Blowing Rock, North Carolina
There are two good routes into Blowing Rock, de-
pending upon the direction you are traveling. If you
are heading south, take U.S. Highway 321 toward
Blowing Rock and turn right onto U.S. Highway 21
Business. This is an easy ride into town. For those
traveling north, the best way into Blowing Rock is to
take the U.S. Highway 221 exit before Moses H. Cone.
It is a leisurely ride back and forth from Julian Price
by this route. Blowing Rock has two notable restaurants. Tijuana Fats is great for Mexican food while the
Blowing Rock Cafe has a wide variety of excellent
dishes.

Alpine Village Inn (704)295-7206 $–$$
Appalachian Motel (704)295-3380 $$
Azalea Garden Inn (704)295-3272 $$
Blowing Rock Inn (704)295-7921 $$
Boxwood Motel (704)295-9984 $$
Hemlock Motel (704)295-7987 $$
Maple Lodge Bed & Breakfast (704)295-3331 $$$
(Breakfast is included in the price.)

*Julian Price Memorial Park. Take a bike break and walk around
Prices Lake. Photo by Kathleen Wheeless.*

Meadowbrook Inn (704)295-9341 $$$
Ridgeway Motel (704)295-7321 $$
Sunshine Inn (704)295-295-3487 $$$
(Breakfast is included in the price.)
Boone, North Carolina
Boone is accessible by two routes. The first is via U.S.
Highway 321; it is 7 miles north on this four-lane
highway. Road conditions are fairly good due to the
spaciousness of the road, but traffic can be aggravated
during heavy tourist seasons. There is some downhill
into Boone and, likewise, a fair amount of climbing
back to the Parkway. The other way in is via Flannery
Fork Road for which there are signs just off of the
Parkway between Mileposts 296 and 297. This road
takes you right into the center of Boone. There are a
couple of miles of rough, gravel road, but the road is
paved at least halfway.

Comfort Inn (704)264-0077 $$
Cabana Motel (704)264-2483 $–$$
High Country Inn (704)264-1000 $–$$
Holiday Inn of Boone (704)264-2451 $$–$$$
Sheraton Appalachian Inn (704)262-0020 $$–$$$
Boone Bike & Touring Co. (704)262-5750
This bike shop is located near Appalachian State University in the center of town at 240 East King Street.

294.0   **Moses Cone Memorial Park**
296.9   **Julian Price Memorial Park**
Julian Price has lakeside campsites and fishing. The campground has 129 tent sites and 62 trailer sites. This campground is one of the few winterized Parkway campgrounds which is usually open all year.

Julian Price to Linville Falls

At 5,837 feet, Grandfather Mountain is ever present in this 9-mile section of the Parkway. It is a massive, broad mountain that watches over the entire Boone and Blowing Rock area. Heading south from Julian Price, with Grandfather Mountain looming ahead, you are approaching the engineering masterpiece of the Park Service, the Linn Cove Viaduct. Cycling across the Linn Cove Viaduct is a real thrill.

The viaduct winds around Grandfather Mountain in partial suspension. The road was built away from the mountain with supports underneath. As you cycle across you can see streams that flow underneath the viaduct. You can almost reach out and touch hemlock and rhododendron. Rather than whizzing past on to your next destination, you can gain a finer appreciation of the vegetation of the area, and the construction of the viaduct, by hiking at least part of the trail that runs parallel to the viaduct.

The viaduct is not a difficult ride. The toughest part of this section is the unrelenting five miles preceding the Linn Cove Viaduct. It doesn't look all that bad, but the grade is considerable.

Once past the viaduct, you may want to stop at the Grandfather Mountain Overlook to reflect upon what you have just passed through. If you are traveling north, the view as you approach Grandfather is spectacular.

Grandfather Mountain is an excellent sidetrip off of the Parkway. Privately owned, the land is protected as a natural habitat for black bear, deer, and other wildlife. At the top of the mountain there are picnic areas, a gift shop and restaurant, and the famous suspension bridge. As you stand in the middle of the bridge, you can feel the wind's destructive power. Winds on top of Grandfather have been known to gust well past 100 miles per hour.

Pineola is the next town of note just off the Parkway with restaurants, a motel, campground, and a post office. From Pineola, the Parkway levels out for four to five miles into a straightaway. The

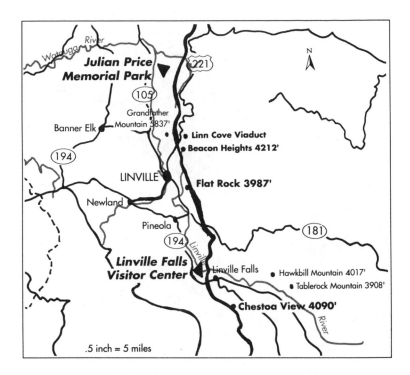

presence of these level stretches always amazes us, especially in the midst of such mountainous terrain.

You are now approaching the Linville Gorge Wilderness Area. You could spend weeks hiking this wild, rugged area. If you are on a mountain bike, the forest service roads that circle the gorge are some of the steepest we have ever cycled. From the campground at Linville Falls, it is well worth a hike to the upper and lower falls. There are views of the gorge and the surrounding Linville Mountain, Hawksbill Mountain, Table Rock, and Jonas Ridge, composed of quartzite, and you are amidst a geological history that goes back to the dinosaur days.

The Linville River attracts fly fishermen to this visitor center and campground. The river runs alongside the campsites on one side of the campground.

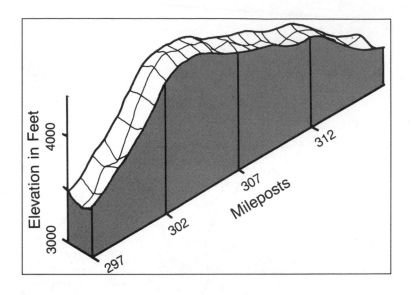

Milepost

298.6   **Holloway Mountain Road**
This road takes you to U.S. Highway 221 which was
formerly the official Parkway route before the viaduct
was completed. There are a few stores less than a mile
down Holloway. This is an easy trip on a bike from
Julian Price campground.
The Poor Mountaineers
Look for this store which stocks groceries and souve-
nir items on the right.
Grandfather Mountain Country Store (704)295-7606
At the intersection of Holloway Mtn. Road and U.S.
Highway 221, this store has a good selection of
groceries and home-baked cakes and cookies. Lunch is
served here also.

304.4   **Linn Cove Viaduct Visitor Center** (elev. 4,315 ft.)
This visitor center and comfort station was built to
accommodate the popularity of the Linn Cove Via-

The magnificent Linn Cove Viaduct. Photo by Kathleen Wheeless.

duct. The Tanawha trail begins here. Facilities include restrooms, telephones and a gift shop. There is a ranger on duty.

305.9 **Grandfather Mountain**
Take U.S. Highway 221 and proceed 3 miles to Grandfather Mountain. Privately owned and operated, facilities are open daily April 1 through November 15 and on winter days (weather permitting). Admission is $6.00 for adults, $3.00 for children. The road to the summit is extremely steep.

312 **Pineola, North Carolina**
Take Highway 181 1.6 miles into Pineola. There is a slight descent into town. You will find restaurants, a post office, and accommodations here.

A stone bridge near Pineola exemplifies the artistry of Joseph M. Troitina, a stonecutter from Spain who crafted most of the walls, tunnels, and overlooks along the Parkway. Photo by Elizabeth Skinner.

Pineola Inn (704)733-4979 $$
Down By The River Campground (704)733-5057

316.3   **Linville Falls Visitor Center**
Trails to Linville Falls and the gorge start here. There is parking and access to the Linville River here also.

316.3   **Linville Falls Campground** (elev. 3,250 ft.)
This Park Service campground was closed and undergoing extensive repairs in the summer of 1989. The campground is scheduled to be open by the 1990 season. The campground has 55 tent sites and 20 trailer sites.

317.4 **Linville Falls, North Carolina**
Linville Falls has several motels and restaurants. The entrance to the Linville Gorge Wilderness Area is 3 miles off the Parkway, from U.S. Highway 221 onto Highway 183, just beyond the town proper.
Parkview Motor Lodge & Restaurant
(704)765-4787 $
Just 500 feet south of the Parkway on U.S. 211.
Linville Falls Motel (704)765-2658 $-$$
This motel is one-half mile off of the Parkway.

Linville Falls to Crabtree Meadows

This is a wonderful area from which to make day trips. You could set up base camp at Linville Falls or Crabtree Meadows and have plenty of options for exploring by bicycle. The various motels in Little Switzerland all make wonderful weekend getaways.

One of the highlights of this area is the vast apple orchard between Mileposts 328 and 329. In the fall, you can buy quite an assortment of apples, including Stayman Winesap, Stark's Delicious, and York Imperial. If you are lucky enough to cycle through here between late April and early May, the apple blossoms will intoxicate you with their perfume.

Highway 226 intersects the Parkway at Milepost 330. A sidetrip to Spruce Pine may not be necessary, but you can find grocery stores, restaurants, motels, and banks here. The Museum of North Carolina Minerals is located at this intersection. Time spent with the exhibits will give you an appreciation of the geology and mineralogy of the Blue Ridge. Displays of amethyst, quartz, emerald, mica, and other rocks and minerals native to the Blue Ridge explain the fascination rock hounds have with the area.

Little Switzerland is a pleasant sidetrip right off of the Parkway at Milepost 334. There are three excellent motels here. This is a good place to treat yourself. Beyond this point heading south there are very few accommodations until you reach Asheville. If you like to browse in shops, there are several good ones in Little Switzerland.

Little Switzerland Tunnel begins the start of many tunnels from here to Cherokee. You may want to mount a lighting system from here on out. If nothing else, a flashing belt beacon on your rear alerts cars to your presence.

Crabtree Meadows has a campground, a restaurant, and a camp store. These are the last facilities on the Parkway proper until Mt. Pisgah, which is 70 tough miles away. There is no other campground right off of the Parkway until Mt. Pisgah. We recommend getting a

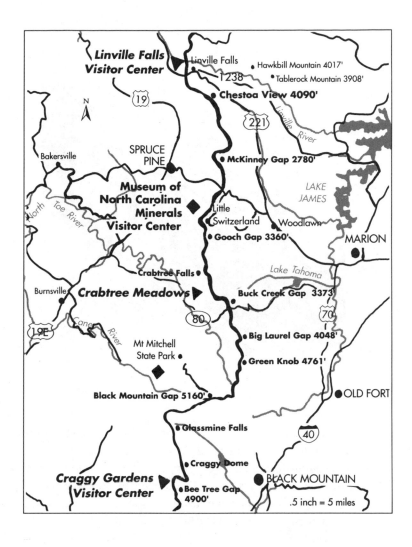

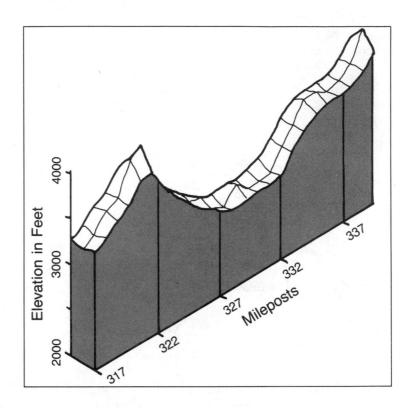

motel room in Asheville so you can get cleaned up and fresh for the grueling climb from Asheville to Mt. Pisgah.

Enjoy the fantastic descent you get in this section. From Chestoa View (elevation 4090 feet) you will drop down to 2,819 feet at Gillespie Gap. That's almost ten miles of pure down. From Gillespie Gap you will begin a climb into the Black Mountains, which culminates with Mt. Mitchell at 6,684 feet.

Milepost

324.8   **Bear Den Family Campground** (704)765-2888
                Take Bear Den Mt. Road six-tenths of a mile to the

Apple trees in full bloom at Skylark Orchard, Milepost 326. Photo by Elizabeth Skinner.

campground. Be on the lookout for this road. Since the campground cannot advertise on the Parkway, there is no sign. Beware of a steep gravel road to the campground. This campground is well managed with showers, laundry, and a camp store.

331   **Museum of North Carolina Minerals**
This Park Service facility is a museum featuring excellent exhibits of area rocks and minerals. A bookstore, restrooms, and drinking water are available here.

331   **Highway 226 intersects here.**
Spruce Pine, North Carolina
Spruce Pine is a whopping 6 miles from the Parkway. There is a shopping center and a motel 3.5 miles from

Chestoa View Overlook offers an outstanding view of Linville Gorge, Table Rock, Hawksbill and Grandfather Mountain. Photo by Elizabeth Skinner.

the Parkway. There are two major grocery stores, a drug store, hardware store, banks, and restaurants here.

331   Pine **Valley Motel** (704)765-6276 $$
You can take a back way into Little Switzerland via Highway 226. If you turn left and go under the bridge you will find a motel and convenience store.
Mountain View Motel (704)765-4233 $

333.4   Little Switzerland Tunnel (542 ft.)

334   Little Switzerland, North Carolina
You might want to call it an early day and hang out for the afternoon.
Alpine Inn (704)765-5380 $
This motel is the furthest from the Parkway, but it is dear to our hearts. It has the most reasonable rates, too. Turn right onto Highway 226A and travel 1 mile.
Big Lynn Lodge (704)765-4257 or (800)654-5232 $$$ Actually, this is a reasonable place to stay when you consider that a hearty dinner and breakfast are included in the price.
Chalet Lodge & Restaurant (800)654-4026 $$-$$$
This elegant lodge was established in 1910. If you're ready for a little pampering, this is the place. Wonderful views of the valley are below.
Sandwich Gallery & Switzerland Store
On the way to the Alpine Inn, you can get gourmet deli sandwiches here.

336.8   **Wildacres Tunnel** (330 ft.)

339.5   **Crabtree Meadows**
Crabtree Meadows has a Park Service campground, a restaurant, and a camp store stocked with basic grocery items. This is a wonderful campground. There are 71 tent sites and 22 trailer sites. Our only wish is that the restaurant open earlier than 9:30 A.M. for breakfast. With a major climb to Mt. Mitchell ahead, breakfast is a must. Crabtree Falls is a 40-minute walk from the campground. Restaurant hours: 9:30 A.M.–6 P.M. daily.

Crabtree Meadows to Craggy Gardens

How big of a deal can one mountain be? Just ask anyone who has done the annual Assault On Mt. Mitchell. If you are undertaking the Parkway in a big way, you owe it to yourself to cycle to the top of Mt. Mitchell. You don't want to deny yourself the opportunity of being able to say you've cycled up to the highest peak east of the Mississippi River. The gain in elevation on the 4.8-mile spur road to the summit is 1,390 feet. The view is unparalleled. The descent is nerve-tingling. The damage to the spruce and fir forests by the woolly aphid and acid rain should be witnessed. Motorists will think you are crazy, but Mt. Mitchell is a bicyclist's mecca.

For those wondering what the Assault on Mt. Mitchell is all about, it's a 102-mile endurance event open to anyone crazy enough to try it. Sponsored by the Spartanburg Freewheelers, the event begins in Spartanburg, South Carolina in late May or early June. In 1989 there were over 1,600 participants. Unfortunately, the event is endangered. Too many participants overtaking the narrow, winding roads of Highway 80 and the Blue Ridge Parkway have the Park Service uneasy about the feasibility of the event. For more information, contact the Spartanburg Freewheelers, P.O. Box 6171, Spartanburg, South Carolina 29304, or call (803) 578-3171.

Camping at Mt. Mitchell State Park allows you a chance to experience the harsh weather conditions characteristic of the higher elevations. These campsites are not fully exposed, but they are situated on the side of the mountain. Mist or rain is likely. The gusting winds characteristic of the mountain are sure to whip your little nylon tent all through the night. There are only nine sites here and they are fairly primitive. Don't expect asphalt leading up to your tent pad. Arrive before noon in order to get one of these precious sites.

The Parkway is spectacular from Mt. Mitchell to Craggy Gardens. You are in the midst of the Black Mountains and they deliver. This entire area is a cyclist's dream. Granted, you have to work extremely

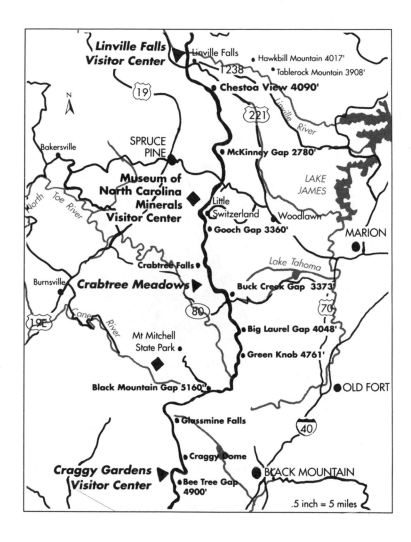

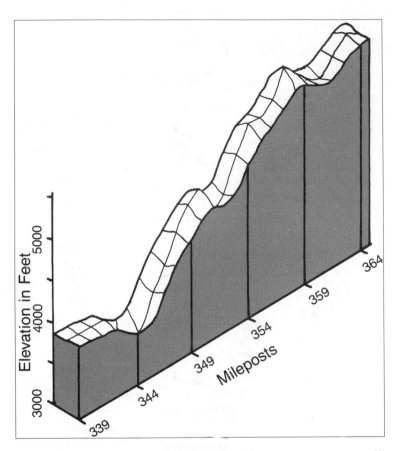

hard, but that always serves to heighten the experience. We would feel cheated if we drove in a car through this area. Once you've traveled the Parkway on a bike, you don't want to do it any other way.

Craggy Gardens is known for its rhododendron. Hiking trails take you to the top of the bald where the view of the Black Mountains is supreme. In addition to rhododendron, mountain laurel, blueberry, mountain cranberry, and mountain ash are all in abundance. Mountain ash grab your attention in the late fall, after the leaves have fallen, when their brilliant red berries provide the only bright color.

Riders line up in downtown Spartanburg for the start of the 14th annual Assault On Mt. Mitchell. Photo by Elizabeth Skinner.

Milepost

344 **Highway 80 intersects here.** There are just a few facilities within close range to recommend.

Mountain Cove Campground & Trout Pond (704)675-5362
One mile north of the Parkway on Highway 80.

Carolina Hemlock Recreation Area
This Pisgah National Forest campground has a bracing mountain stream that feeds a deep swimming pool, but it is 6 miles north toward Burnsville. Cycling to Carolina Hemlocks from Crabtree Meadows or Little Switzerland and back makes an outstanding day trip.

Hamrick Inn Bed & Breakfast (704)675-5251 $–$$
This bed & breakfast is 1.5 miles on Highway 80 toward Burnsville. Breakfast is included in the price.

Fatigued riders two miles from the top of Mt. Mitchell — it's been a grueling day. Photo by Elizabeth Skinner.

	Hamrick Resort RV Park & Campground is adjacent to the inn.
344.5	**Twin Tunnel (North) (300 ft.)**
344.7	**Twin Tunnel (South) (401 ft.)**
349.0	**Rough Ridge Tunnel (150 ft.)**
355.4	**Mount Mitchell State Park**

The road to the summit is a 5-mile climb with grades reaching 33 percent. This is much steeper than any other grade on the Skyline Drive and the Parkway. Actually, the first two miles to the summit are steeper than the last three. There's a snack bar, Natural History Museum, and observation tower at the top.

The campground is 4 miles from the Parkway. Remember, there are only nine campsites and they are first-come, first-served. There is a restaurant here also, but it has sometimes been closed during the peak season. Restaurant hours: Monday–Friday 11 A.M.–8 P.M.; Saturday–Sunday 8 A.M.–8 P.M.

364.4   **Craggy Pinnacle Tunnel** (245 ft.)
364.5   **Craggy Gardens** (elev. 5,640 ft.)
Craggy Gardens has a visitor center with restrooms and drinking water. There is also a good selection of literature on the Blue Ridge. Take a hike to Craggy Dome, Craggy Pinnacle, and Craggy Knob.

Craggy Gardens to Asheville

Get ready for some fun! You have a solid 10 miles of spectacular down into Asheville. You'll gain it back if you are cycling on to Mt. Pisgah, but for now, enjoy. Pisgah National Forest spreads its lush blanket of green as far as the eye can see. The Swannanoa River Valley and the town of Black Mountain are to the east.

Known as "The Land of the Sky," Asheville is the quintessential city of the Blue Ridge. With a population of 160,000, it has become an urban center in its own right. Its burgeoning size warrants some careful directions on how to get around. We suggest you take one of two routes to reach the inner city. Town Mountain Road leads to downtown Asheville and two bike shops. The route through Biltmore Forest situates you best for the Biltmore Estate. A third route is best for reaching the airport. We outline each route below.

Of modern design in wood and stone, the Folk Art Center sits serenely in its mountain setting. If you appreciate fine handicrafts, you will want several hours to spend here. Bring your credit card, because the artsy jewelry, hand-loomed fabrics, and original pottery are expensive. The Folk Art Center also has an extensive selection of books on the southern highlands.

There are numerous tourist attractions in Asheville. The Biltmore Estate, the Thomas Wolfe Memorial and home, and the seasonal festivals held in Asheville are all reasons to spend some time in the city. If you plan on touring Asheville, you may want to write the Asheville Travel and Tourism Office for detailed information.

Milepost

365.5	**Craggy Flats Tunnel** (400 ft.)
374.4	**Tanbark Ridge Tunnel** (780 ft.)
377.4	**Craven Gap** (elev. 3,132 ft.)
	Highway 694 intersects here. Two of the Asheville bike shops recommend exiting the Parkway here to

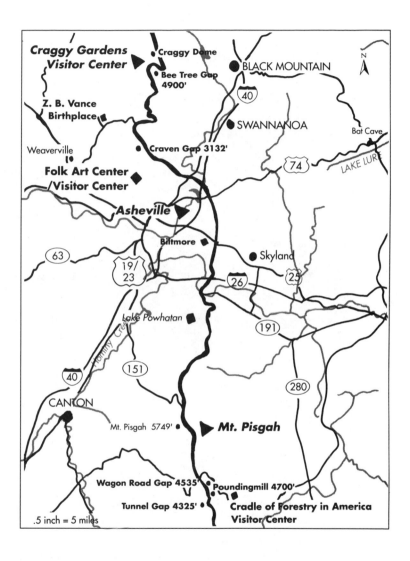

reach their shops. Exiting the Parkway via Town
Mountain Road places you in downtown Asheville.
There are also several motels in this area. The route to

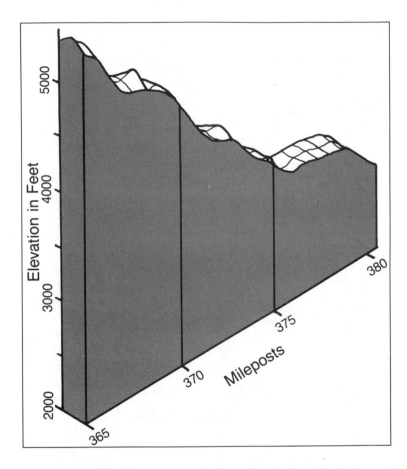

Pro Bikes passes several motels which we list below.
Pro Bikes of Asheville (704)253-2800
Hours: Monday–Friday 9 A.M.– 6 P.M.; Saturday 9 A.M.–
3 P.M.; closed Sunday.
Take Highway 694 (Town Mountain Road) at Craven
Gap 6.5 miles to College Street. Town Mountain Road
is a two-lane scenic highway which winds through a
residential area. From the Parkway, Town Mountain
Road climbs for about a mile and then descends the

mountain into Asheville. Traffic is light, but there are several switchbacks so be careful. Turn right onto College Street. At the second traffic light, turn right onto Oak Street; bear left onto Woodfin Street. (Oak Street turns into Woodfin Street.) At the second light, turn right onto U.S. Highway 25 North (Merrimon Avenue.) Follow U.S. Highway 25 North through three traffic lights. Pro Bikes will be on the left. The address is 342 Merrimon Avenue. The total distance to Pro Bikes from the Parkway is 8 miles.

Sheraton Inn (704)253-1851 or (800)325-3535 $$$
The Sheraton Inn is located en route to Pro Bikes on 22 Woodfin Avenue.

American Court (704)253-4427 $$
American Court is located en route to Pro Bikes on 85 Merrimon Avenue.

Downtown Motel (704)253-9841 $
Also along this route is Downtown Motel at 65 Merrimon Avenue.

J. M. Hearn & Company (704)253-7851
Hours: Monday-Saturday 8:30 A.M.–5:30 P.M.; closed Sunday.
This bike shop also recommends following Highway 694 to reach their shop. J. M. Hearn is directly downtown. Getting to this shop is a little less complicated than to Pro Bikes. Follow Highway 694 (Town Mountain Road) 6.5 miles to College Avenue. Turn right at College Avenue. Follow College Avenue to Broadway and turn right. Total mileage from the Parkway to J. M. Hearn is 7.5 miles. The address of J. M. Hearn is 34 Broadway.

382 **Folk Art Center**
Operated by the Southern Highland Handicraft Guild, this is a required stop for anyone interested in crafts, books, or history and information on the Blue Ridge.

Restrooms and drinking water are available here.

382.5   **U.S. Highway 70 intersects here.**

The closest facilities are just 1 mile east on U.S. Highway 70 toward Black Mountain. There are numerous motels and several restaurants.

Cricket Inn (704)298-7952 $–$$

Days Inn East (704)298-5140 $$

Econo Lodge (704)298-5519 $$

Holiday Inn East (704)298-5511 $$

Heading west toward Asheville, you will find a grocery store, post office, banks, and a medical facility. Asheville Medical Center is located 1.3 miles from the Parkway on U.S. Highway 70 West.

383.5   **I-40 crosses underneath the Parkway.**

384.7   **U.S. Highway 74 intersects here.**

Avoid this interchange. There is nothing here of note.

388.1   **U.S. Highway 25 intersects here.**

Biltmore Estate

At the U.S. Highway 25 South exit, we found a beautiful route into the tourist area of Asheville. Biltmore Estate is only 4 miles via this route. En route you get to cycle through one of the most elegant neighborhoods in Asheville. Take the U.S. Highway 25 South exit and turn left into Biltmore Forest. Take an immediate right onto Stuyvesant Road. Follow this road about 2 miles until it merges onto Vanderbilt Road. You will bear right here. Vanderbilt Road ends at the Biltmore Dairy Bar, which features delicious ice cream. It is 3.6 miles from the Parkway to the Dairy Bar. Biltmore Estate is a quarter mile to your left from the light. You are in the midst of Biltmore Village which has numerous gift shops. There are several motels in the area.

Quality Inn Biltmore (704)274-1800 $$$

The Quality Inn is adjacent to the Biltmore Dairy Bar.

Howard Johnson Lodge (704)254-2300 $$-$$$
Visible from the Dairy Bar, right on Hendersonville
Road.
Plaza Motel (704)274-2050 $$
Left from the Dairy Bar on Hendersonville Road.

388.1   U.S. **Highway 25 South** is our recommended exit for
the Asheville Airport and the third bike shop, **Liberty
Bicycles.**
You can take U.S. Highway 25 into Asheville, but it is
a well-traveled, two-lane highway. There are major
shopping centers within a quarter mile of the Parkway
in either direction on U.S. Highway 25.
Liberty Bicycles (704)684-1085
Hours: Monday–Friday 10 A.M.–6 P.M.; Saturday 10
A.M.– 4 P.M.; closed Sunday.
Take U.S. Highway 25 South toward Hendersonville
just 2.5 miles. The shop is on the right, set back from
the road. Look for signs.
Asheville Airport
Follow U.S. Highway 25 South to Airport Road. Turn
right onto Airport Road and follow to airport. This
entire area is congested. U.S. Highway 25 South is a
four-lane highway.

393.6   **French Broad River** (elev. 2000 ft.)
Highway 191 intersects the Parkway here. There are
picnic areas along the river just off of the Parkway in
both directions. There are a few facilities on Highway
191 north, but this is a narrow, two-lane highway.
There is a convenience store eight-tenths of a mile
from the Parkway.
Lake Powhatan Recreation Area
This Pisgah National Forest campground is quite a
detour from the Parkway. It's only 3 miles off of the
Parkway, but that's 3 miles mostly downhill.

Asheville to Mt. Pisgah

There are nine tunnels in this 15-mile section, ranging in length from 275 to 1,320 feet. Pine Mountain Tunnel at Milepost 399.3 is the longest on the Parkway. Let your imagination run wild with the names of the tunnels as you travel through them: Buck Spring, Ferrin Knob, Grassy Knob, Young Pisgah Ridge, Fork Mountain ... you'll need the diversion with all of the climbing you've got to do. From Milepost 384 to Milepost 408 you will climb 3,705 feet. You may have to get off your bike and cry, but you'll make it. This is why Asheville is such a good break point for cyclists doing extended tours. Whether you are traveling north or south, you will have a climb out of Asheville. Take heart if you are touring the Parkway north to south. The climb from Asheville to Mt. Mitchell is worse, at a grand total of 4,265 feet climbed to the entrance of Mt. Mitchell State Park.

At Milepost 399.7 you might want to stop and view Pisgah Ridge rising up to Mt. Pisgah, whose peak is at 5,749 feet. You will be traveling across Pisgah Ridge because the Parkway follows it for 24 miles to Tanasee Bald. At Tanasee Bald the Parkway enters the Great Balsam Range.

The historic presence of the Vanderbilts is evident upon reaching Mt. Pisgah. In the late 1800s, George Washington Vanderbilt bought up 130,000 acres of land in the area, including Mt. Pisgah. Remnants of a stone foundation are all that are left of Vanderbilt's mountain retreat at Buck Spring Gap.

Pisgah Inn is truly a mountain retreat. It hugs the side of the mountain, and the floor-to-ceiling picture windows in the dining room and each of the guest rooms look out to views of the hazy-blue ridges toward Hendersonville and Brevard. Pisgah Inn is the place to sample rainbow trout. It is prepared here five different ways.

Camping here is enjoyable; with an excellent store and restaurant dining as an option, you have plenty of resources to fall back on. A day or two spent here is full of possibilities. The steep hike to the magnificent Mt. Pisgah can occupy an entire afternoon. There's a

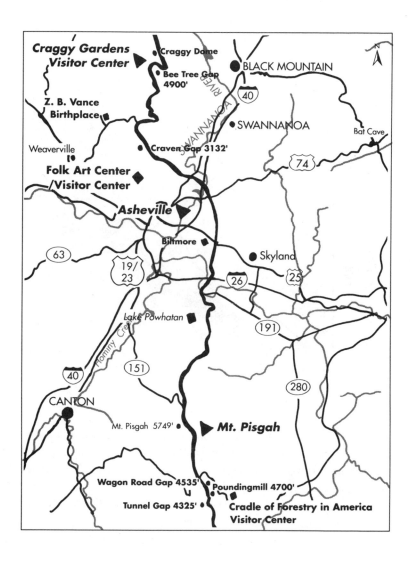

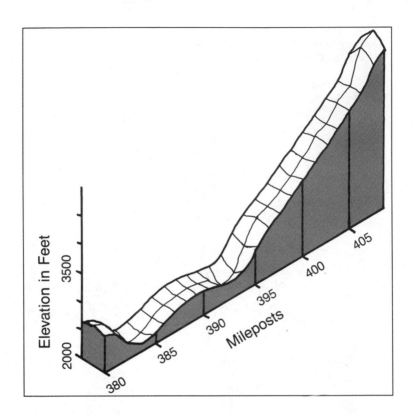

weather station and an observation tower at the summit. It's windy at the top, and weather changes can be sudden, so bring a jacket. Additional hikes, in all directions from the campground, make for plenty of exploring.

Mountain laurel and several varieties of rhododendron, including catawba, Carolina, and rosebay, are abundant in the campground, as well as a couple miles further on the Parkway in the Cradle of Forestry. An overlook at Milepost 410.3 reveals the Pink Beds, part of the Cradle of Forestry area of Pisgah National Forest, which are a dense undergrowth of mountain laurel and rosebay rhododendron interspersed with tiny mountain bogs. Late May through June is the time to find the rhododendron and laurel in bloom. Wildflowers are prolific all summer throughout the campground and the grounds surrounding the inn.

Milepost

397.1	**Grassy Knob Tunnel** (770 ft.)
399.1	**Pine Mountain Tunnel** (1434 ft.)
	This is the longest tunnel on the Parkway.
400.9	**Ferrin Knob Tunnel No. 1** (561 ft.)
401.3	**Ferrin Knob Tunnel No. 2** (421 ft.)
401.5	**Ferrin Knob Tunnel No. 3** (375 ft.)
403.0	**Young Pisgah Ridge Tunnel** (412 ft.)
404.0	**Fork Mountain Tunnel** (389 ft.)
406.9	**Little Pisgah Tunnel** (576 ft.)
407.3	**Buck Springs Tunnel** (462 ft.)
407.8	**Mt. Pisgah Picnic Area** (elev. 4,900 ft.)
408.6	**Pisgah Inn** (704)235-8228 $$–$$$
	Pisgah Inn's reputation precedes it. Reservations are strongly suggested. At the very least, treat yourself to a meal here. You deserve it after your crazy cycling antics. You will also find telephones and a camp store here.
408.8	**Mt. Pisgah Campground** (elev. 4,850 ft.)
	The campground adjoins Pisgah Inn. The campground has 70 tent sites and 70 trailer sites. The restaurant and an adequate camp store provide options for food.

Mt. Pisgah to Cherokee

It is 60 rugged miles to Cherokee, and you had better be well prepared. Facilities are scarce in these parts. You will be cycling along Pisgah Ridge to the Great Balsams. You will reach the highest point on both the Skyline Drive and the Blue Ridge Parkway at Richland Balsam, elevation 6,053 feet. Stop here and take it all in. You have truly come far if you have cycled from Front Royal to this point. It is a major achievement to get here from Cherokee or Asheville.

"Awesome" describes this section of the Parkway. From Mt. Pisgah, the first geologic feature to command your attention is Looking Glass Rock. Its prominent, bare granite dome has become quite famous. After five or six preliminary miles of ups and downs, the Parkway begins the long ascent to Richland Balsam. Graveyard Fields and Graveyard Ridge are eerie in their barren, flat appearance described as "bog-like" because of their lack of trees. In 1925 a forest fire destroyed 25,000 acres of spruce-fir forest. Sixty years later, the forest is slowly recovering. The "fields" are now filled with blueberries, mountain laurel, rhododendron, and bush honeysuckle.

It could be argued that the best way to appreciate this area is by foot. Much of these mountains is accessible only by hiking trails. The Shining Rock Wilderness Area is 13,400 acres of wild mountain terrain. A spur road at Milepost 420.2 takes you to Ivestor Gap where the hiking trails begin. You might have time to take a brief hike to the top of Devil's Courthouse, by way of the trail at Milepost 422.4, on your way to Cherokee. When mists hug this rocky, rugged summit it looks devilish for sure.

The manner in which the trees grow in this section is something you can appreciate as you make the arduous climb to Richland Balsam. Fraser fir and red spruce are symbols of these mountains. They are the true inhabitants, able to survive the brutal climate of higher elevations. The one disturbing thing about cycling through Richland Balsam is the sight of the dead Fraser fir that cover the

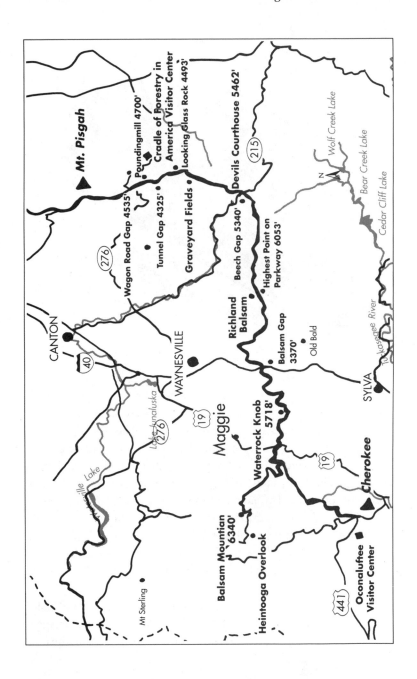

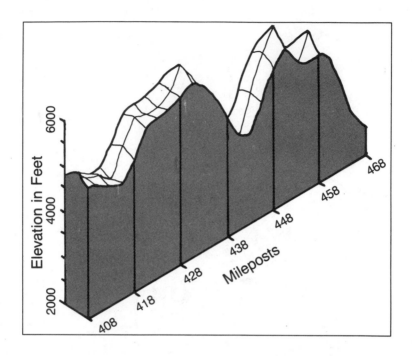

highest peaks. Just as with Mt. Mitchell, the Fraser fir is dying because of an insect called the Balsam Woolly aphid and other environmental stresses such as acid rain. It is hoped that, ultimately, the Fraser fir will be able to genetically adapt to this parasite.

Logic would follow that since you have just cycled to the highest point on the Parkway then, surely, you will now have a great descent. Well, you do. You also have a climb back up to Waterrock Knob before the final descent into Cherokee. The grand total of elevation climbed in this entire stretch is 6,225 feet. For those cycling from Cherokee to Mt. Pisgah, you will have to endure a total climb of 9,305 feet. The major portion of this climb, 7,470 feet, is from Cherokee to Richland Balsam.

There has been some debate over which direction is tougher for cyclists, north to south or south to north. The general consensus is that the Parkway is tougher traveling south to north. In fact, the total

The authors at 6,053 feet. Photographer unknown.

feet climbed is higher in this direction, but not by much: 48,722 feet versus 48,601 feet. See Appendix B for details.

What options do you have if you can't cycle this section in a single day? Well, Balsam Mountain campground isn't a lot of help. The spur road up to it climbs an additional 1,100 feet, and all you've got left is a 10-mile descent into Cherokee. Your single alternative for lodging and food is the exit toward Waynesville at Balsam Gap, Milepost 443.1. This is an easy down toward the town of Balsam where you will find food, a motel, and a campground. Aside from this, the only feasible exit we know of is at Soco Gap. Any other way off of the Parkway involves a major descent and too many miles detoured off of the Parkway.

The descent into Cherokee is a bicyclist's dream. Don't get carried away in the tunnels. They are much more dangerous when you are traveling at top speeds. There are six tunnels between Soco Gap and Cherokee.

Milepost

410.1   **Frying Pan Tunnel** (577 ft.)

411.9   **Wagon Road Gap** (elev. 4,535 ft.)
U.S. Highway 276 intersects here.
Cradle of Forestry in America Visitor Center
It is a steep 4-mile descent from the Parkway on
U.S. Highway 276 South. If your base camp is Mt.
Pisgah, this would be a good sidetrip. The visitor
center has exhibits, a movie, and interpretive trails
and is open daily from 10 A.M. to 6 P.M. An entrance
fee is charged.

422.1   **Devil's Courthouse Tunnel** (665 ft.)

431.4   **Richland Balsam Overlook** (elev. 6,053 ft.)
Highest point on the Blue Ridge Parkway.

439.7   **Pinnacle Ridge Tunnel** (813 ft.)

443.1   **U.S. Highway 23-74**
Balsam Motel (704)456-3637 $
Turn left at Balsam exit, proceed one half mile on
U.S. Highway 23-74.
Balsam, North Carolina (elev. 3,370 ft.)
Go south at Balsam exit on U.S. Highway 23-74,
turn left at sign for Balsam and go one half mile.
Moonshine Creek Campground (704) 586-6666
Hot showers.
Balsam Mountain Inn (704) 456-9498 $$$
Elegant accommodations complete with library,
porches, great room, country breakfast, lunch and
dinner.
Bicycle Outfitters (704) 456-5663
Bicycle Outfitters is located in Waynesville which
is seven miles on U.S. Highway 23-74. Take the
Balsam exit off the Parkway and proceed on U.S.
Highway 23-74 South. Take the Waynesville exit
onto Highway 276 South. Proceed toward down-
town Waynesville. Turn right on Branner Ave.

The Parkway heads out away from Mt. Pisgah. Looking Glass Rock is visible to the left. Photo by Charlie Skinner.

Bicycle Outfitters is .1 mile on the left at 411 Branner Ave.

451.2   **Waterrock Knob Parking Overlook** (elev. 5,718 ft.) You will find restrooms and drinking water here.

455.7   **Soco Gap** (elev. 4,340 ft.) U.S. Highway 19 intersects here. It is 5 miles straight down to Maggie Valley on a two-lane highway. **Starvin Marvin Service Station** (704)926-3635 This convenience store is just three-tenths of a mile on U.S. Highway 19 South. Although primarily a trailer park, they do allow tent camping here.

458.2   **Balsam Mountain Campground** (elev. 6,340 ft.) The campground at Balsam Mountain is part of the Great Smoky Mountain National Park. Take Heintooga Spur Road 8.6 miles to the campground with a gain in elevation of 1,100 feet. There are forty campsites here. Facilities include drinking water and comfort stations. The road is paved.

Devil's Courthouse Tunnel — one of many between Asheville and Cherokee. Photo by Elizabeth Skinner.

458.8	**Lickstone Ridge Tunnel** (402 ft.)
459.3	**Bunches Bald Tunnel** (255 ft.)
461.2	**Big Witch Tunnel** (348 ft.)
465.6	**Rattlesnake Mountain Tunnel** (395 ft.)
466.2	**Sherrill Cove Tunnel** (550 ft.)
469.1	**End of the Blue Ridge Parkway** (elev. 2,020 ft.)

For the record, the Parkway is actually 470 miles long. The Linn Cove Viaduct altered the total mileage. There are no immediate plans to change the mileposts.

469.1   **Cherokee, North Carolina** (elev. 2,020 ft.)

You are now connected with the Great Smoky Mountains National Park. It is 2 miles south to Cherokee by way of U.S. Highway 441.

Cherokee Campground (704)497-9838

To get to this private campground take U.S. Highway

441 South to U.S. Highway 19 North and go 2 miles.
Showers and laundry are available.

Cherokee KOA (704)497-9711
On U.S. Highway 441 South take first left to Big Cove
Road and follow signs 4 miles to campground. You'll
find a pool and a camp store here.

Comfort Inn (704)497-2411 $–$$$
One half mile west of Cherokee on U.S. Highway 19.

Holiday Inn Cherokee (704)497-9181 $$–$$$
Newfound Lodge (704)497-2746 $$
On the Oconaluftee River located 1 mile from the
Parkway entrance on U.S. Highway 441 North.

Qualla Motel (704)497-5161 $$–$$$
Located on U.S. Highway 441 South.

Riverside Motel & Campground (704)497-9311 $$
Located three-quarters of a mile south of Cherokee on
U.S. Highway 441.
Waterfront rooms and campsites.

Great Smoky Mountains National Park
You can continue on for 33 miles from Cherokee to
Gatlinburg through the Great Smoky Mountains
National Park on U.S. Highway 441. The road is
similar in character to the Parkway. The highest
elevation on the road through the Smokies is 5,048
feet at Newfound Gap. The campgrounds in Great
Smoky Mountains National Park have a reputation
for filling up quickly, so arrive early. Gatlinburg is
loaded with motels and restaurants.

Smokemont Campground
Smokemont is just 3.8 miles from the southern
terminus of the Parkway. Exit right onto U.S. 441.
Call 1-800-365-CAMP to make reservations.
You can continue on for 33 miles from Cherokee to
Gatlinburg through the Great Smoky Mountains
National Park on U.S. Highway 441. The road is

similar in character to the Parkway. The highest
elevation on the road through the Smokies is 5,048
feet at Newfound Gap. The campgrounds in Great
Smoky Mountains National Park have a reputation for
filling up quickly, so arrive early. Gatlinburg is loaded
with motels and restaurants.

Appendix A:

Bicycle Shops

Although we have already listed bicycle shops in our point-by-point description, we thought a directory organized by city would be helpful for anyone needing a quick reference.

Front Royal, Virginia
* Mike's Bike & Hobby Shop (703)635-5864
  Mike's is located a quarter mile from the Skyline Drive in the Royal Plaza Shopping Center.

Waynesboro, Virginia
* Rockfish Gap Outfitters (703)943-1461
  Rockfish Gap Outfitters is 3 miles west on Highway 250 heading into Waynesboro. In case of emergencies, use telephone number on the door of the store.

Roanoke, Virginia
* Cardinal Bicycle (703) 345-1687
  Cardinal Bicycle is located on Orange Avenue (Highway 460 East) in Roanoke. The Vinton, Virginia exit off the Parkway affords the best access. See detailed directions under Vinton, Virginia.

Boone, North Carolina
* Boone Bike and Touring Co. (704)262-5750
  Boone Bike and Touring is located in the center of town near Appalacian State University on 240 East King Street.

Asheville, North Carolina
* J. M. Hearn & Company (704)253-7851
  J. M. Hearn is located in downtown Asheville. For detailed directions to the shop see the descriptive section from Craggy Gardens to Asheville.

- Liberty Bicycles (704)684-1085
  Take the Highway 25 South exit off of the Parkway heading toward Hendersonville. Travel 2.5 miles. Look for signs. The shop is set away from the road on the right.
- Pro Bikes of Asheville (704)253-2800
  Pro Bikes is centrally located near downtown Asheville. For detailed directions to the shop see the descriptive section from Craggy Gardens to Asheville.

Waynesville, North Carolina
- Bicycle Outfitters (704) 456-5663
  Bicycle Outfitters is located 7 miles off the Parkway in Waynesville. For directions see the entry on Balsam, North Carolina at Milepost 443.1.

As you can see, there are a mere six cities with bike shops spread out over 570 miles. Preventive maintenance is in your best interest.

Appendix B: For More Information

For maps and information on the Skyline Drive and Shenandoah National Park write:

Superintendent
Shenandoah National Park
Luray, VA 22835
(703)999-2266

A brochure listing additional books and maps on Shenandoah National Park may be obtained by writing:

Shenandoah Natural History Association
Luray, VA 22835

For a directory of facilities in and surrounding Shenandoah National Park write:

Shenandoah Valley Travel Association
P.O. Box 1040, Department TG88
New Market, VA 3132
(704)740-3132

For maps and information on the Blue Ridge Parkway write:

Superintendent
Blue Ridge Parkway
700 Northwestern Plaza
Asheville, NC 28801
(704)259-0769

For a directory of facilities along the Blue Ridge Parkway write:

Blue Ridge Parkway Association, Inc.
P.O. Box 453
Asheville, NC 28802

State Tourism Offices:
 Virginia Division of Tourism
 202 North Ninth Street
 Richmond, VA 23219
 1-800-VISIT-VA

 Division of Travel and Tourism
 North Carolina Department of Commerce
 430 North Salisbury Street
 Raleigh, NC 27611
 1-800-VISIT-NC

Chambers of Commerce

District of Columbia

Washington:
 District of Columbia Chamber of Commerce
 1411 K. Street N.W.
 Washington, D.C. 20005
 (202) 347-7201

Maryland

Baltimore:
 Greater Baltimore
 Committee
 111 S. Calvert Street #1500
 Baltimore, MD 21202
 (301) 727-2820

North Carolina

Asheville:
 Asheville Area Chamber of
 Commerce
 151 Haywood Street
 P.O. Box 1010
 Asheville, NC 28802
 (704) 258-3858

Black Mountain:
 Black Mountain-Swannanoa
 Chamber of Commerce
 201 East State Street
 Black Mountain, NC 28711
 (704) 669-2300

Blowing Rock:
Blowing Rock Chamber of
Commerce
P.O. Box 406
Blowing Rock, NC 28605
(704) 295-7851

Boone:
Boone Area Chamber of
Commerce
350 Blowing Rock Road
Boone, NC 28607
(704) 264-2225

Brevard:
Brevard Area Chamber of
Commerce
35 West Main Street
P.O. Box 589
Brevard, NC 28712
(704) 883-3700
(800) 648-4523

Burnsville:
Yancey County Chamber of
Commerce
2 Town Square, Rm. #3
Burnsville, NC 28714
(704) 682-7413

Cherokee:
Cherokee Chamber of
Commerce
P.O. Box 465
Cherokee, NC 28719
(800) 222-6157 NC
(800) 438-1601 U.S.

Maggie Valley:
Maggie Valley Area Chamber
of Commerce
Hwy 19 Stallard Shopping
Mall
P.O. Box 87
Maggie Valley, NC 28751
(704) 926-1686
(800) 334-9036

Sparta:
Alleghany County Chamber
of Commerce
915 N. Main Street
P.O. Box 1237
Sparta, NC 28675
(919) 372-5473

Spruce Pine:
Mitchell County Chamber of
Commerce
Rt.1 Box 796
Spruce Pine, NC 28777
(704) 765-9483
(800) 227-3912

West Jefferson:
Ashe County Chamber of
Commerce
P.O. Box 31
West Jefferson, NC 28694
(919) 246-9550

Virginia

Charlottesville:
Charlottesville-Albemarle
County Chamber of Com-
merce
5th & East Market Street
P.O. Box 1564
Charlottesville, VA 22902
(804) 295-3141

Front Royal:
Front Royal-Warren County
Chamber of Commerce
501 South Royal Avenue
P.O. Box 568
Front Royal, VA 22630
(703) 635-3185

Galax:
Galax-Carroll-Grayson
Chamber of Commerce
405 North Main Street
Galax, VA 24333
(703) 236-2184

Luray:
Page County Chamber of
Commerce
46 East Main Street
Luray, VA 22835
(703) 743-3915

Roanoke:
Roanoke Regional Chamber
of Commerce
14 West Kirk Avenue
P.O. Box 700
Roanoke, VA 24004-0700
(703) 983-0700

Staunton:
Staunton-Augusta County
Chamber of Commerce
30 North New Street
Staunton, VA 24401
(703) 886-2351

Vinton:
Vinton Chamber of Com-
merce
119 Lee Avenue
P.O. Box 83
Vinton, VA 24179
(703) 343-1364

Waynesboro:
Waynesboro-East Augusta
Chamber of Commerce
301 West Main Street
Waynesboro, VA 22980
(703) 949-8203

Appendix C:
Major Uphills
And Elevations Climbed,
North and Southbound

This chart, designed by Tom DeVaughn of Troutville, Virginia, provides you with a quick tally of the gains in elevation along the Blue Ridge Parkway. The chart does two things. It divides the Parkway into sections and adds up the total number of feet climbed within sections. It also specifies at what mileposts major uphills begin and end, with the elevation climbed for each uphill. For example, southbound between milepost 4.7 and 8.5 the Parkway has a continuous gain in elevation of 1,100 feet.

Keep in mind that beginning a ride at 3,000 feet and cycling to a destination at 4,500 feet does not mean a simple gain of 1,500 feet. The Skyline Drive and the Parkway both rise and fall any number of times before arriving at certain elevations. You may climb the same 500 feet four or five times without any indication on the National Park Service maps.

While we provide this chart, and the elevation profile charts in the point by point descriptive section, we hope you will not be intimidated by elevation. Try not to dwell on the task. Just take in the scenery and enjoy the subtle changes each 500 feet can make.

Mileposts	Northbound			Southbound		
	Total Elev. Climbed	Major Uphills Mileposts	Elevation Change	Total Elev. Climbed	Major Uphills Mileposts	Elevation Change
0–24	1,450 ft.	13.7–10.7	563 ft.	2,810 ft.	0–3	391 ft.
		9.2–8.5	222 ft.		4.7–8.5	1,100 ft.
		4.7–3.0	300 ft.		9.2–10.7	322 ft.
					18.5–23.0	785 ft.
24.0–48.0	2,670 ft.	46.4–43.9	627 ft.	1,742 ft.	37.4–38.8	229 ft.
		40.0–38.8	331 ft.		42.0–43.9	570 ft.
		37.4–34.0	951 ft.		47.0–48.0	177 ft.
48.0–63.0	1,870 ft.	63.0–49.3	1,852 ft.	250 ft.	48.0–49.3	228 ft.
63.0–76.7	0			3,305 ft.	63.0–76.7	3,305 ft.
76.7–96.0	2,865 ft.	93.1–91.6	374 ft.	1,360 ft.	89.1–91.6	569 ft.
		89.1–87.3	634 ft.		93.1–95.4	428 ft.
		85.6–84.7	230 ft.			
		83.5–76.7	1,490 ft.			
96.0–120.4	2,680 ft.	115.0–113.0	280 ft.	1,657 ft.	118.1–120.4	462 ft.

Mileposts	Total Elev. Climbed	Northbound Major Uphills Mileposts	Elevation Change	Total Elev. Climbed	Southbound Major Uphills Mileposts	Elevation Change
		106.0–103.6	500 ft.			
		102.5–99.8	820 ft.			
120.4						
120.4–144.0	2,006 ft.	140.1–139.3	229 ft.	3,200 ft.	127.0–132.5	1,400 ft.
		136.0–134.9	285 ft.		134.0–134.9	195 ft.
		124.6–123.1	320 ft.		136.4–138.2	275 ft.
		121.4–120.4	265 ft.			
144.0–168.0	1,840 ft.	159.4–157.6	389 ft.	2,530 ft.	150.6–152.1	278 ft.
		150.6–149.8	226 ft.		157.0–157.6	200 ft.
					164.7–168.0	830 ft.
168.0–192.0	2,445 ft.	189.4–188.7	220 ft.	1,745 ft.	169.5–170.1	260 ft.
		175.1–171.9	575 ft.		176.2–177.0	212 ft.
		168.9–168.0	185 ft.		186.6–188.8	360 ft.
192.0–216.0	2,225 ft.	215.6–214.0	260 ft.	2,047 ft.	195.0–196.2	235 ft.

Mill Mountain Spur—length to summit: 3.1 miles. Elevation climbed from Parkway to summit: 580 ft.; elevation climbed from summit to Parkway 330 ft.

	Northbound			Southbound		
Mileposts	Total Elev. Climbed	Major Uphills Mileposts	Elevation Change	Total Elev. Climbed	Major Uphills Mileposts	Elevation Change
216.0–240.0	1,566 ft.	210.6–209.4	222 ft.		197.6–198.7	210 ft.
		199.4–198.7	165 ft.		200.5–201.5	335 ft.
		240.0–239.3	160 ft.	2,530 ft.	216.6–217.7	240 ft.
		238.5–237.2	270 ft.		231.3–233.1	550 ft.
		220.8–220.1	205 ft.		233.7–235.2	280 ft.
240.0–264.6	2,625 ft.	257.8–256.8	200 ft.		235.8–236.9	365 ft.
		248.0–244.5	495 ft.	2,680 ft.	240.0–240.8	170 ft.
		243.8–242.9	270 ft.		249.0–249.8	235 ft.
		242.4–241.5	300 ft.		251.3–252.8	300 ft.
264.6–288.0	3,050 ft.	285.2–283.8	400 ft.		263.6–264.6	360 ft.
		279.6–278.8	270 ft.	3,160 ft.	265.2–266.8	270 ft.
		276.4–273.1	910 ft.		269.8–271.1	330 ft.
		269.8–268.6	315 ft.		271.4–273.1	575 ft.
		268.1–266.8	380 ft.		276.4–277.4	375 ft.
					281.7–282.4	280 ft.

Northbound

Mileposts	Total Elev. Climbed	Major Uphills Mileposts	Elevation Change
288.0–312.0	2,185 ft.	309.9–306.5	460 ft.
		305.6–305.0	200 ft.
		295.8–293.8	555 ft.
		291.8–289.9	275 ft.
312.0–336.3	3,120 ft.	336.3–335.7	215 ft.
		327.4–325.8	290 ft.
		325.0–320.7	1,210 ft.
		316.4–312.4	520 ft.
336.3–358.5	1,705 ft.	351.9–349.9	565 ft.
		334.1–341.8	530 ft.
		339.8–338.9	260 ft.
355.4			

Southbound

Major Uphills Mileposts	Elevation Change	Total Elev. Climbed
282.7–283.8	255 ft.	
286.0–287.8	500 ft.	
288.7–289.9	250 ft.	2,210 ft.
291.8–293.8	400 ft.	
298.6–302.1	1,005 ft.	
316.4–318.2	380 ft.	2,705 ft.
318.5–320.7	590 ft.	
330.9–332.1	410 ft.	
332.6–334.5	545 ft.	
336.3–338.9	540 ft.	4,060 ft.
345.4–349.9	1,480 ft.	
351.9–355.0	920 ft.	
355.4–358.5	520 ft.	

Spur Road to Mt. Mitchell is 4.8 miles in length.
Total elevation climbed from Parkway is 1,390 ft.

		Northbound			Southbound	
Mileposts	Total Elev. Climbed	Major Uphills Mileposts	Elevation Change	Total Elev. Climbed	Major Uphills Mileposts	Elevation Change
358.5–384.0	4,265 ft.	383.5–376.7	1,135 ft.	680 ft.	361.1–364.1	500 ft.
		375.3–364.1	2,535 ft.			
		361.1–358.5	540 ft.			
384.0–408.0	850 ft.	No major uphills.	3,705 ft.		393.8–396.4	920 ft.
					397.3–399.7	430 ft.
					400.3–405.5	965 ft.
					405.7–407.7	745 ft.
408.0–431.4 (431.4 is the Parkway's highest elev.)	1,835 ft.	426.5–424.8	325 ft.	2,775 ft.	416.8–420.2	1,100 ft.
		423.2–421.6	250 ft.		423.2–424.8	230 ft.
		415.6–413.2	385 ft.		426.5–428.2	405 ft.
		411.9–409.6	400 ft.		429.0–431.4	600 ft.
431.4–469.1	7,470 ft.	469.1–462.2	2,240 ft.	3,450 ft.	443.1–451.2	2,450 ft.
		461.6–458.9	1,000 ft.		455.7–458.9	810 ft.
		455.7–451.2	1,480 ft.			

	Northbound			Southbound		
Mileposts	Total Elev. Climbed	Major Uphills Mileposts	Elevation Change	Total Elev. Climbed	Major Uphills Mileposts	Elevation Change
		443.1–435.5	2,020 ft.			
		433.3–431.4	475 ft.			
458.2		Heintooga From Balsam Mtn.			To Balsam Mtn.	
		SpurRoad 3.6–1.0	860 ft.		0.0–1.0	255 ft.
					3.6–8.6	845 ft.

Total Uphill Climb North
48,722 ft.

Total Uphill Climb South
48,601 ft.

Bibliography

The Blue Ridge Parkway Directory, Asheville, NC: Blue Ridge Parkway Association, Inc., 1988.

Catlin, David T. A Naturalist's Blue Ridge Parkway, Knoxville, TN: University of Tennessee Press, 1984.

Ezell, Walter. "Assault On Mt. Mitchell: It's Not a Race," Bicycle Guide 3 April 1986: 38-41.

Heatwole, Henry. Guide to Shenandoah National Park and Skyline Drive, Luray, VA: Shenandoah Natural History Association, 1985.

Jolley, Harley E. The Blue Ridge Parkway, Knoxville, TN: University of Tennessee Press, 1969.

Lord, William G. Blue Ridge Parkway Guide, 4 vols., New York: Eastern Acorn Press, 1982.

Muller, Jean M. and James M. Barker. "Design and Construction of Linn Cove Viaduct," Journal of the Prestressed Concrete Institute 30 Sept./Oct. 1985.

Porter, Eliot. Appalachian Wilderness; the Great Smoky Mountains. Natural and human history by Edward Abbey. Epilogue by Harry M. Caudill. New York: Dutton, 1970.

U.S. Department of Commerce. National Oceanic and Atmospheric Administration. National Environmental Satellite, Data and Information Service. National Climatic Data Center. "Average Climatic Conditions Along the Appalachian Trail For April - October." Asheville, NC: National Climatic Data Center, June 1975.

————. *Comparative Climatic Data For the United States Through 1986*. Asheville, NC: National Climatic Data Center, May 1987.

U.S. Department of the Interior. National Park Service. *Blue Ridge Parkway Log*. Asheville, NC: National Park Service

Worldwide Chamber of Commerce Directory, Washington, D.C.: Worldwide Chamber of Commerce, Inc., 1989.

Index